Audio Access Included 🔊

PAT DONOHUE PLAYS
AMERICAN FINGERSTYLE
GUITAR FAVORITES

T0080183

To access audio visit:
www.halleonard.com/mylibrary

Enter Code
6778-4886-1303-5840

Music transcriptions by Pete Billmann, Ron Piccione and David Stocker

ISBN 978-1-4803-8231-2

For more information on Pat Donohue visit: www.patdonohue.com

HAL•LEONARD®
CORPORATION
7777 W. BLUEMOUND RD. P.O. BOX 13819 MILWAUKEE, WI 53213

In Australia Contact:
Hal Leonard Australia Pty. Ltd.
4 Lentara Court
Cheltenham, Victoria, 3192 Australia
Email: ausadmin@halleonard.com.au

Visit Hal Leonard Online at
www.halleonard.com

from *American Guitar*

Arkansas Traveller

Southern American Folk Song

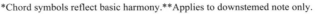

*Chord symbols reflect basic harmony.**Applies to downstemed note only.

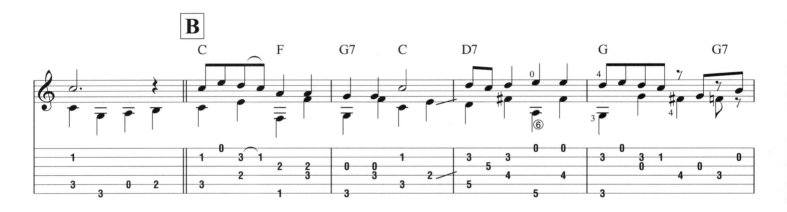

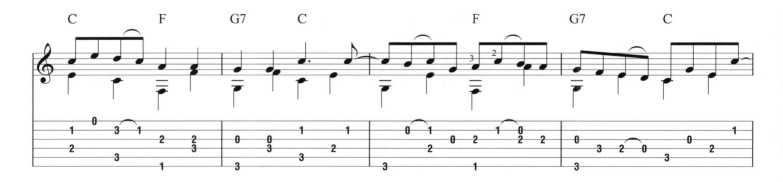

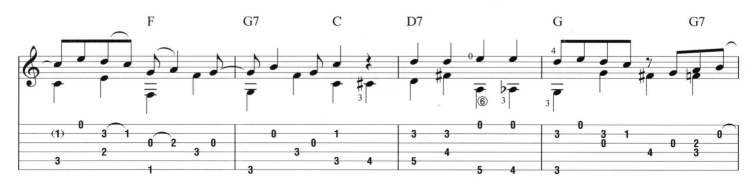

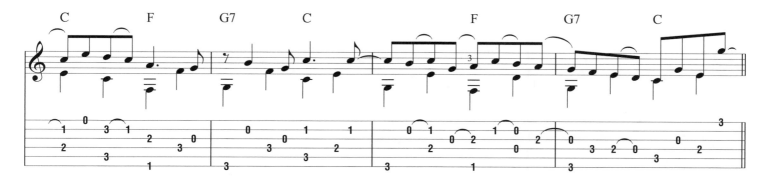

C

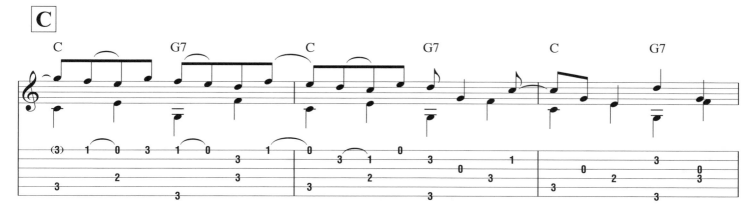

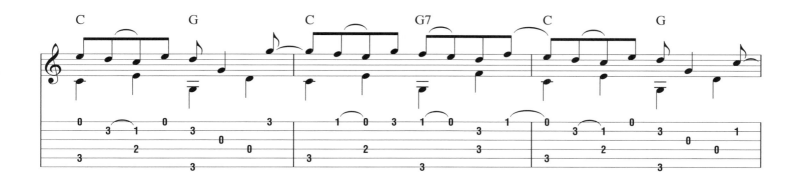

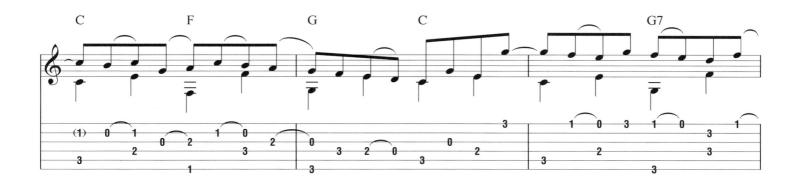

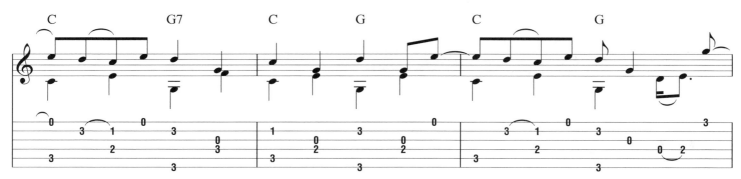

D

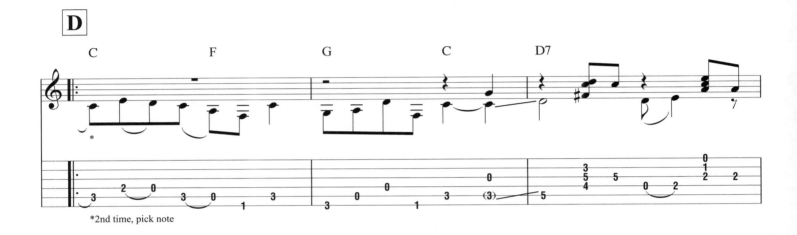

*2nd time, pick note

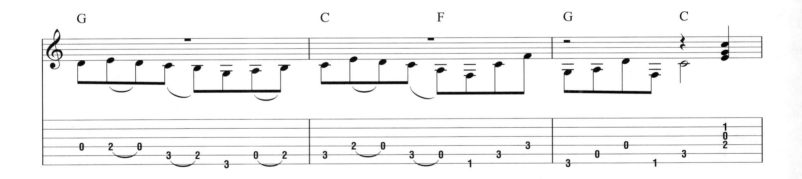

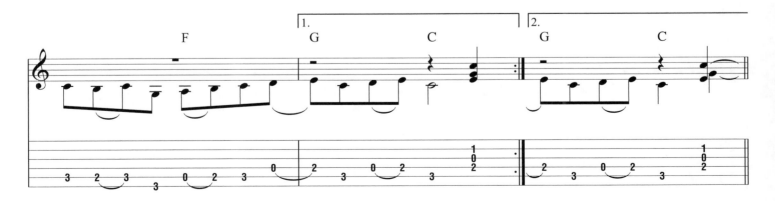

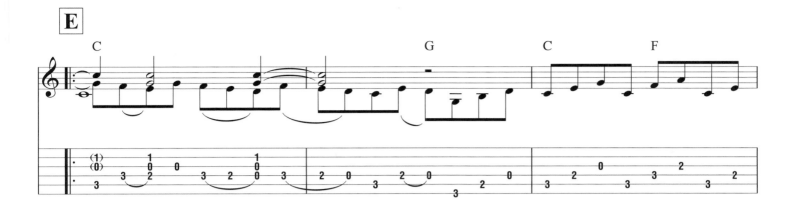

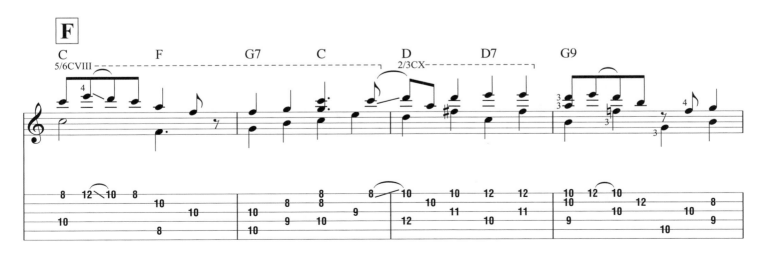

F

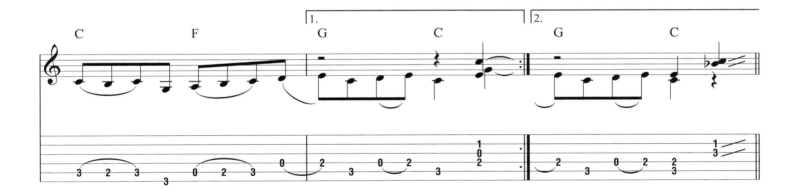

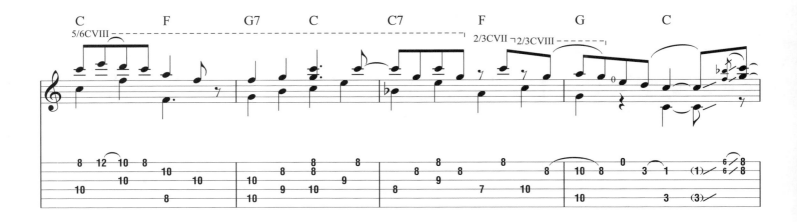

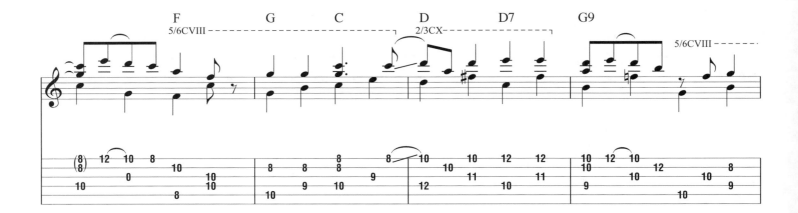

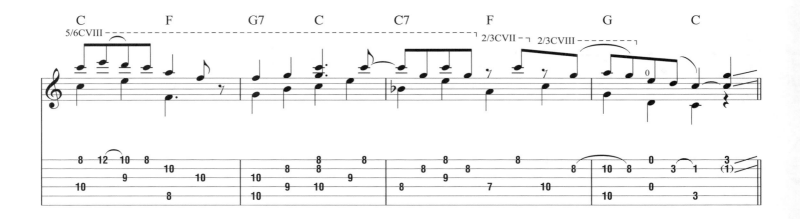

G

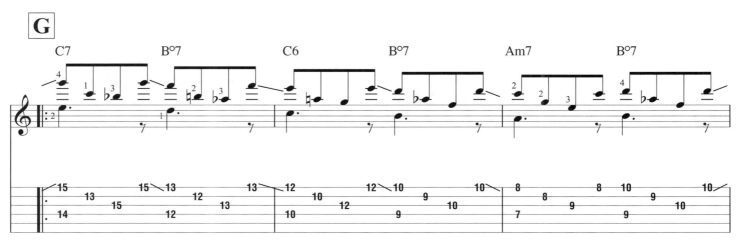

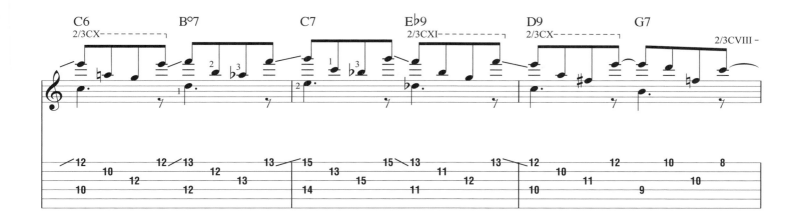

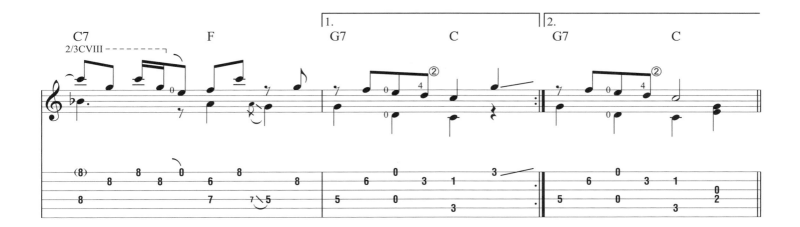

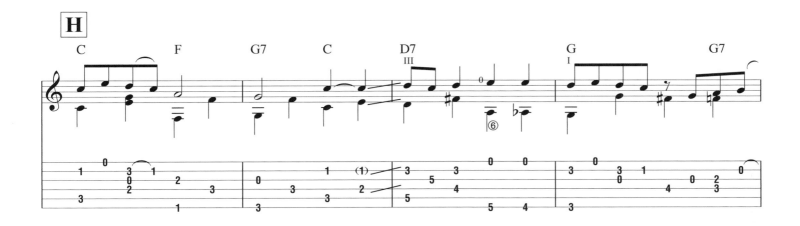

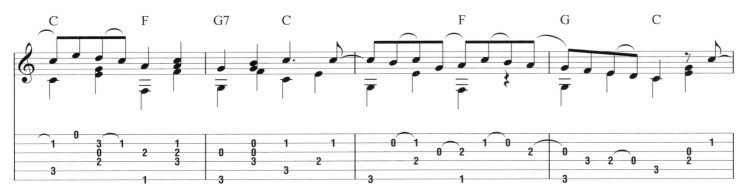

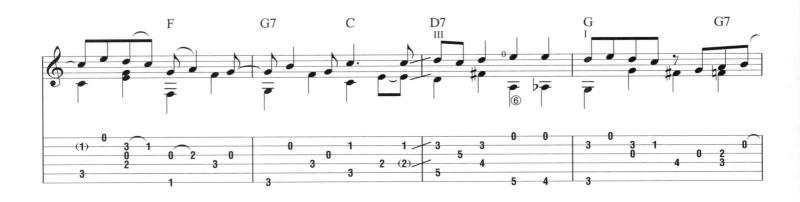

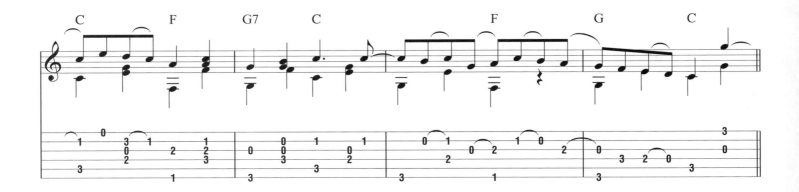

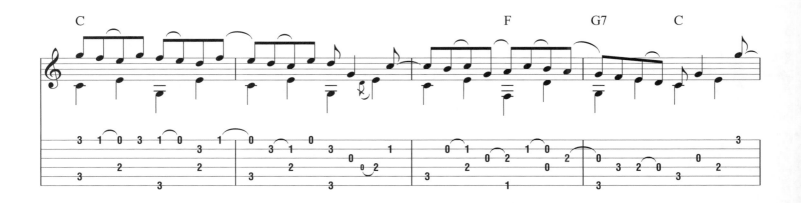

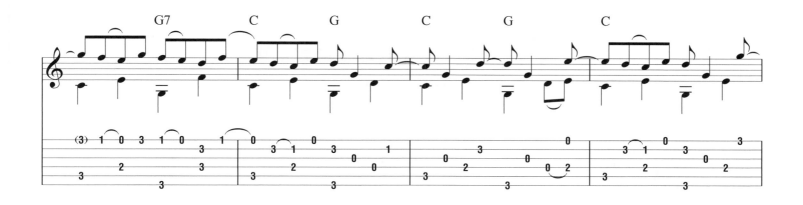

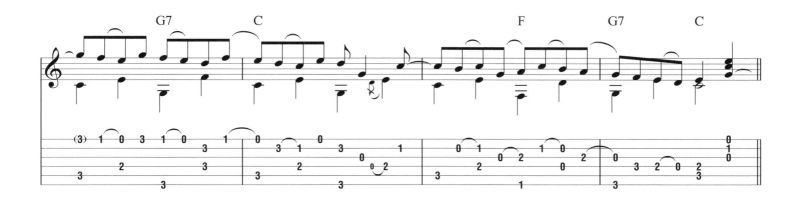

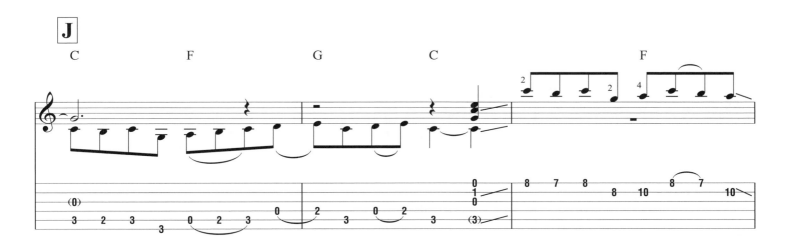

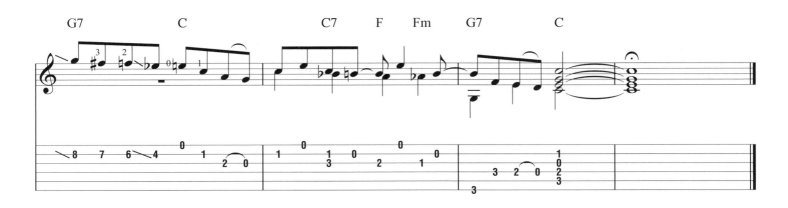

Big Blind Bluesy

By Pat Donohue

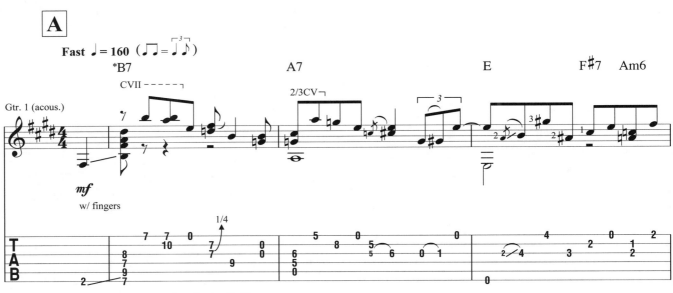

*Chord symbols reflect implied harmony.

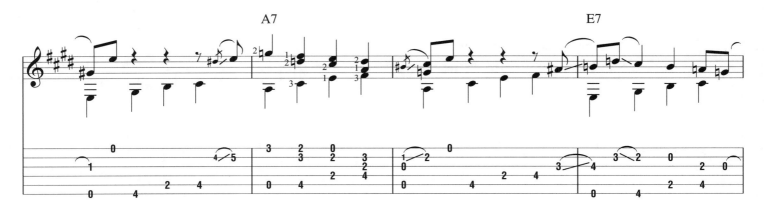

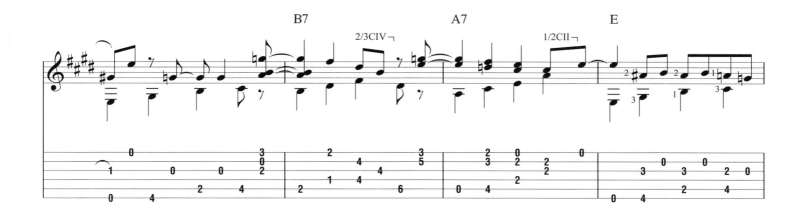

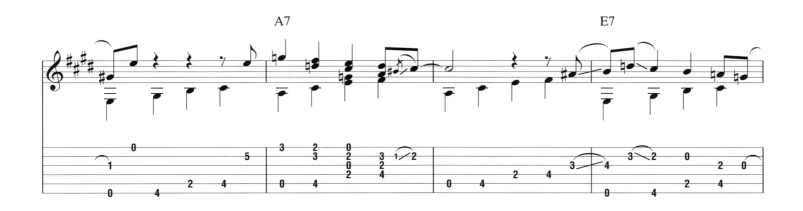

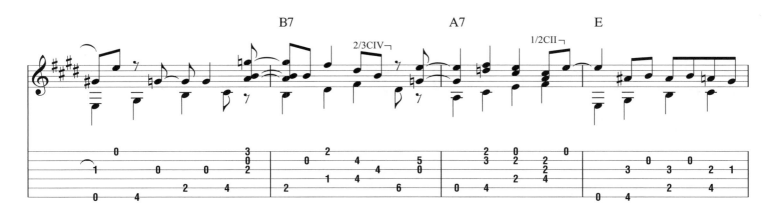

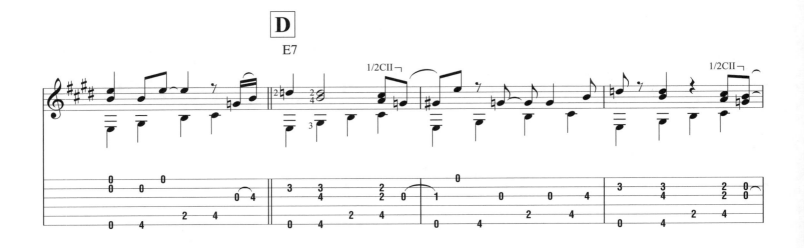

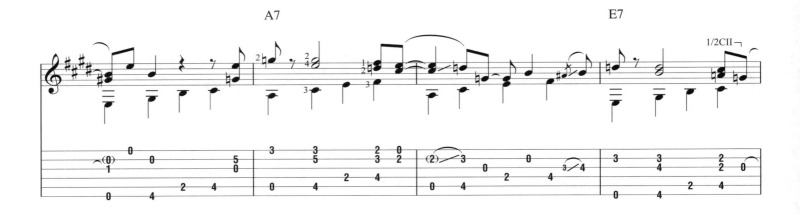

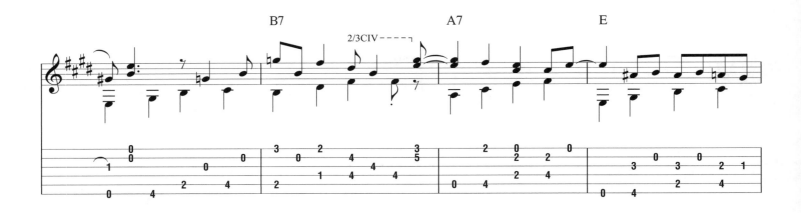

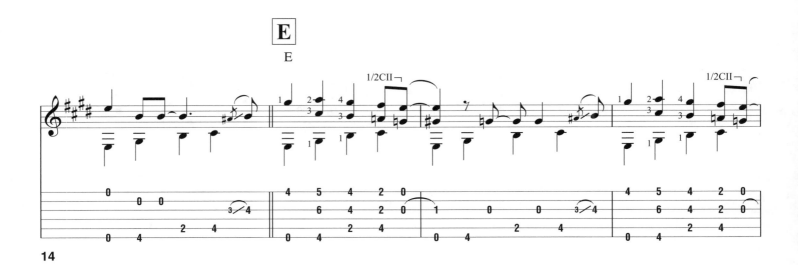

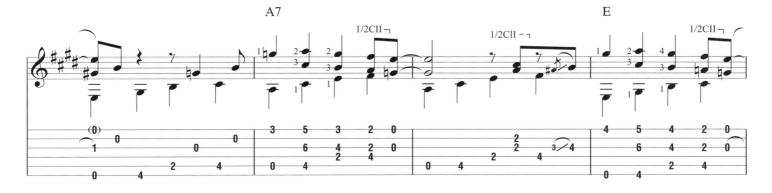

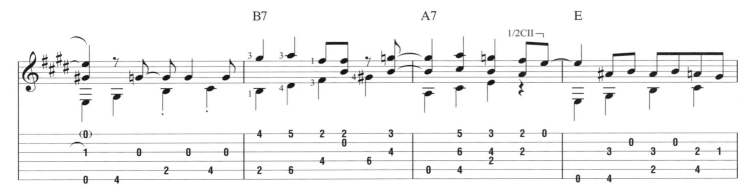

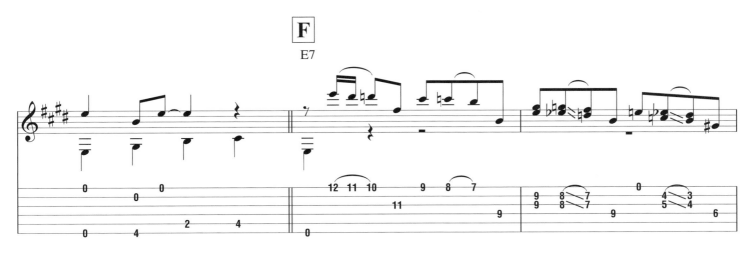

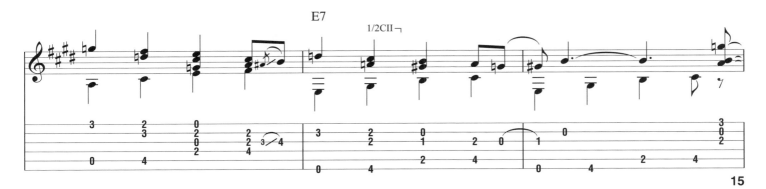

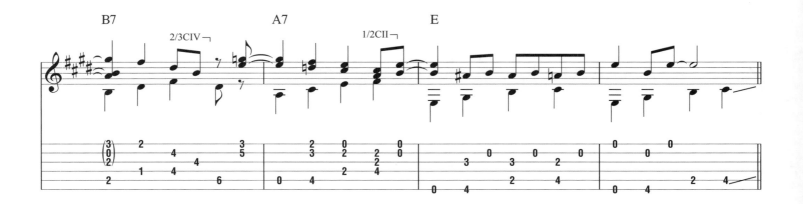

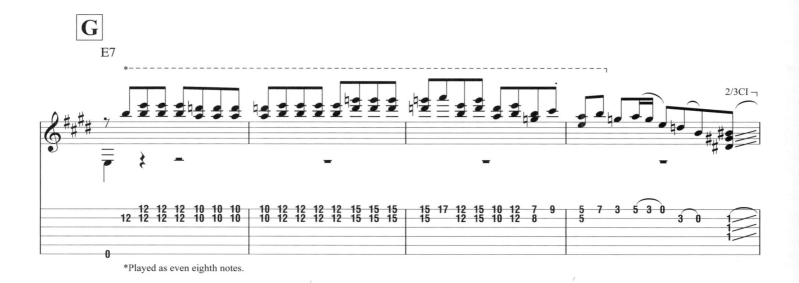

*Played as even eighth notes.

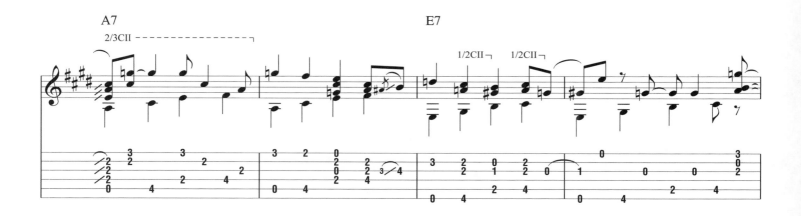

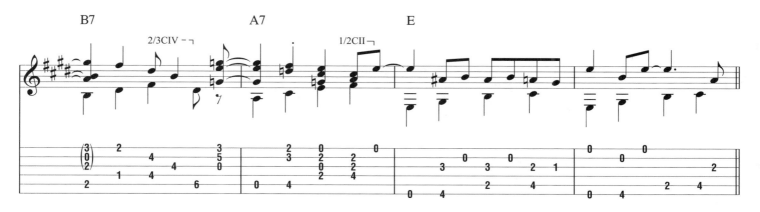

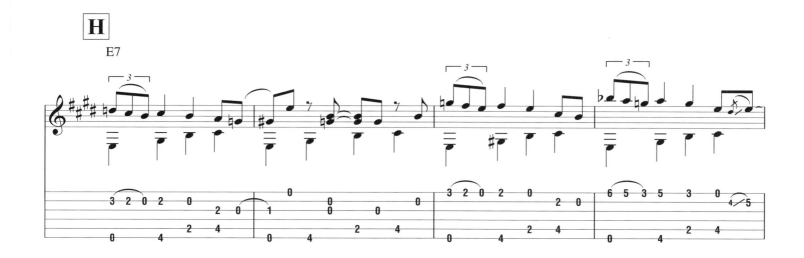

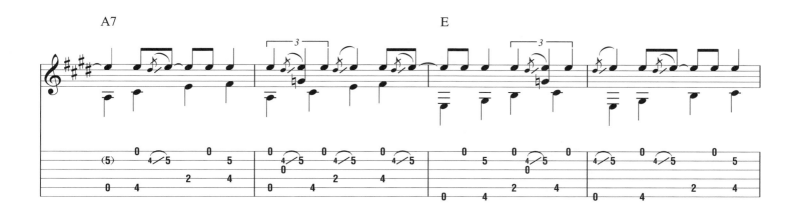

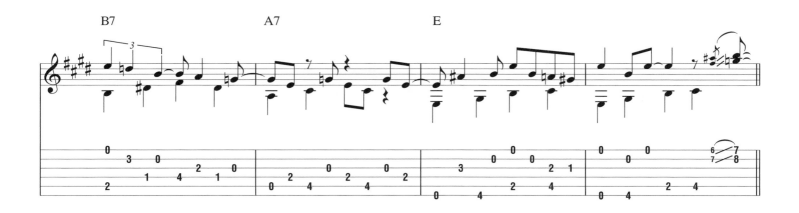

D.S. al Coda

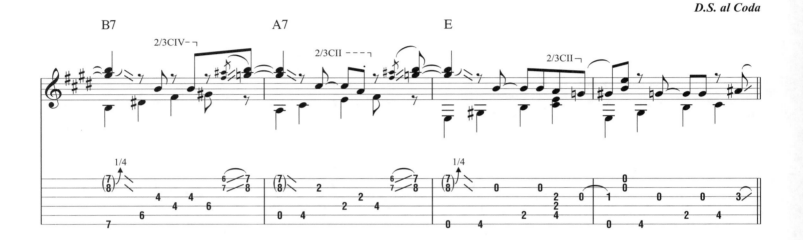

✛ **Coda**

Begin fade

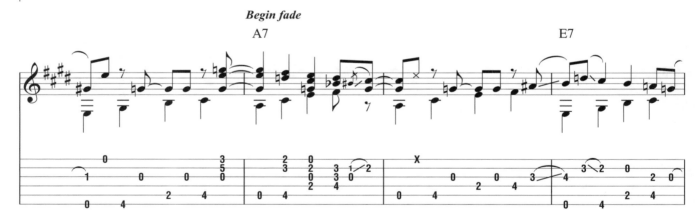

Fade out

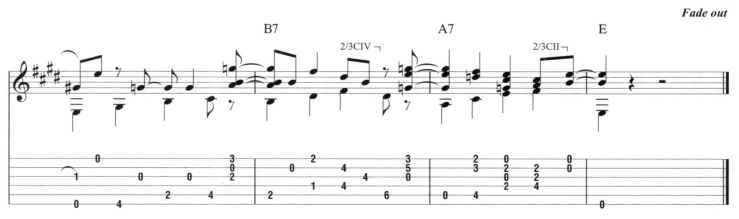

December Waltz

By Pat Donohue

Drop D tuning:
(low to high) D-A-D-G-B-E

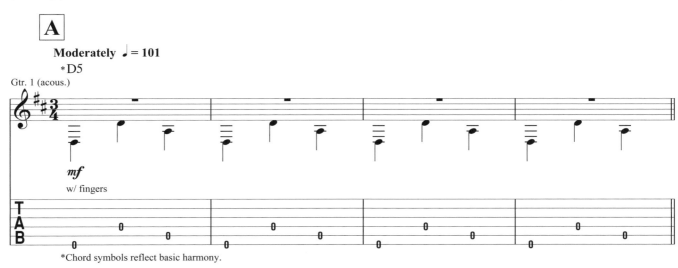

*Chord symbols reflect basic harmony.

**w/ slide

**Wear slide on fourth finger.

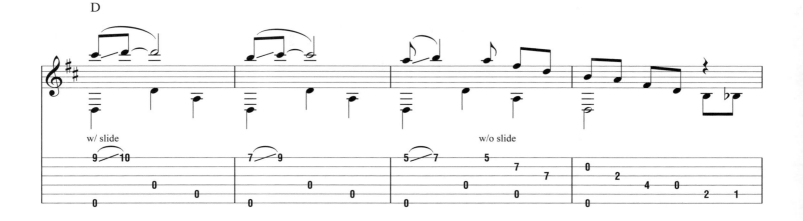

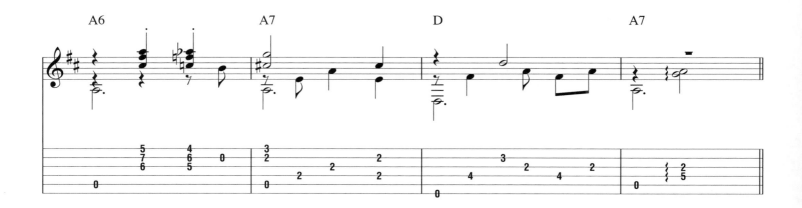

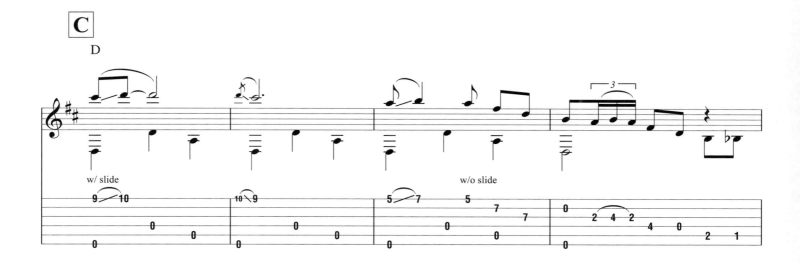

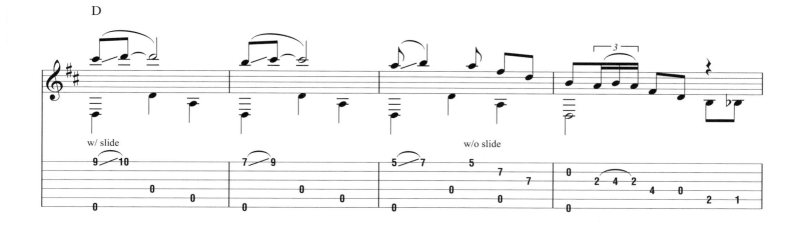

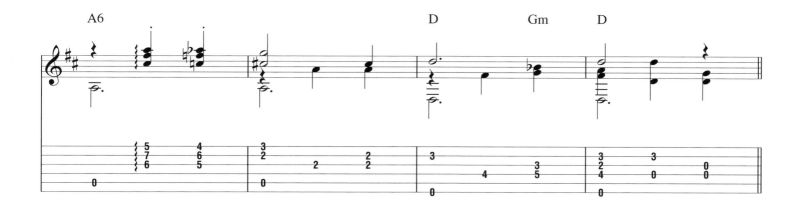

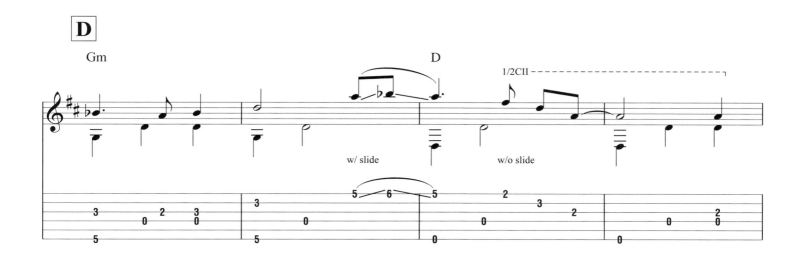

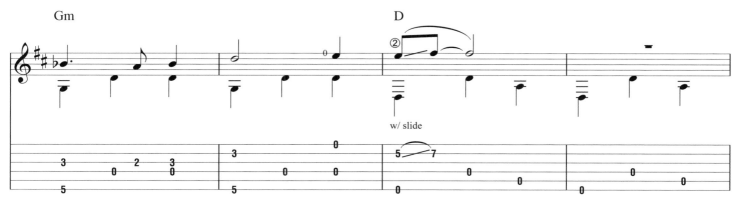

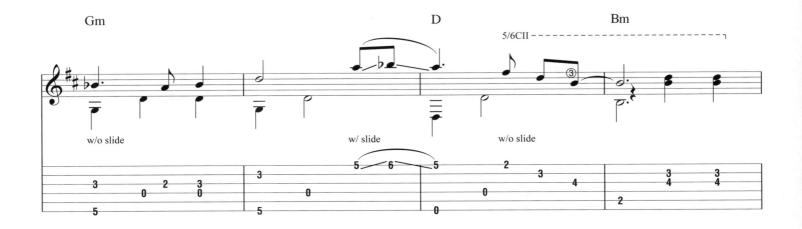

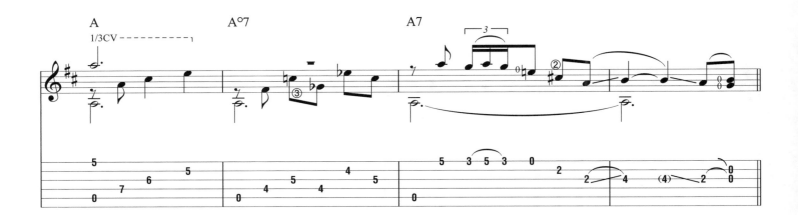

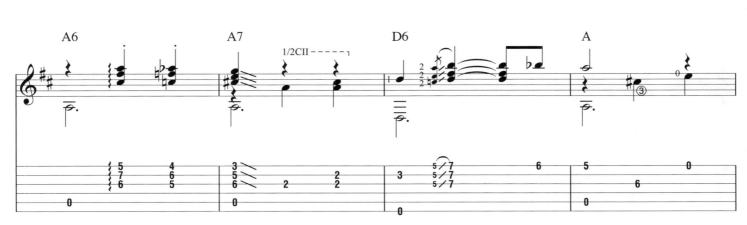

D

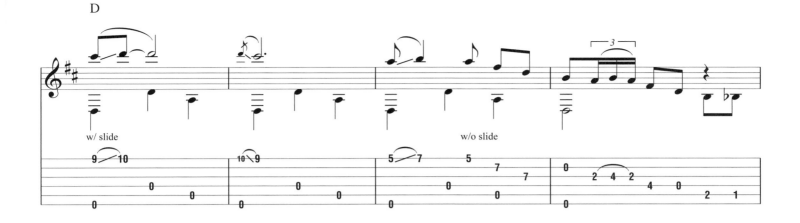

w/ slide   w/o slide

A6   A7   D   Dsus4   D

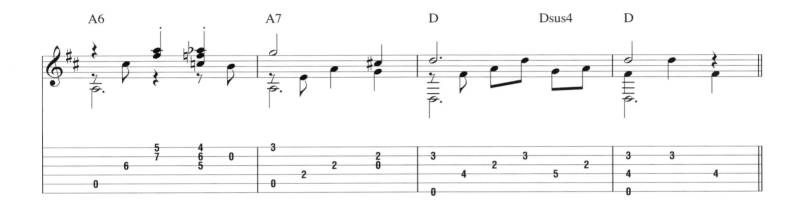

 F

Gm   D

1/2CIII

w/ slide   w/o slide

Gm   D

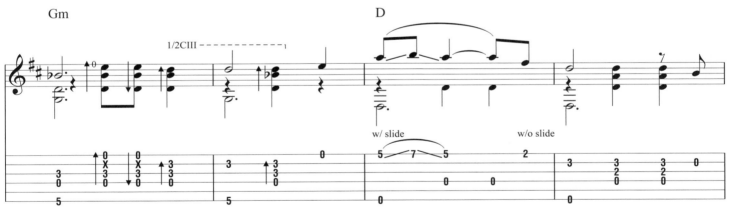

w/ slide   w/o slide

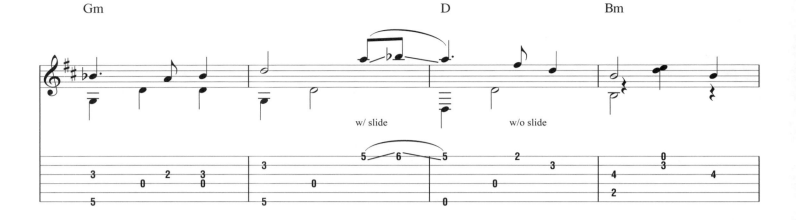

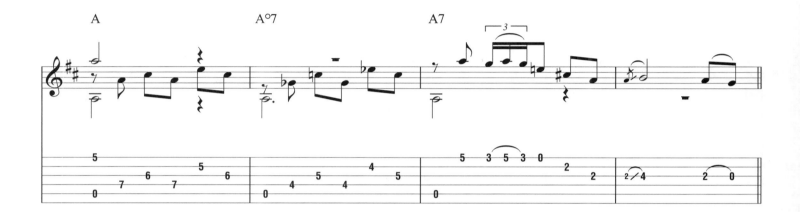

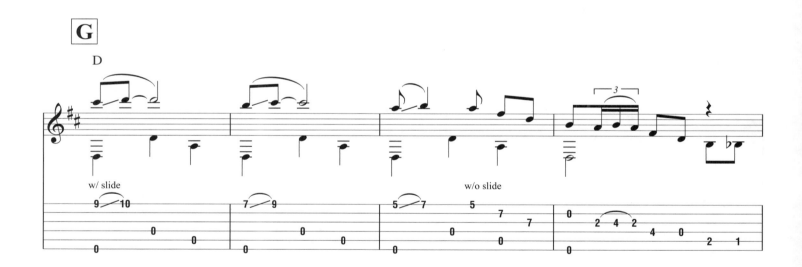

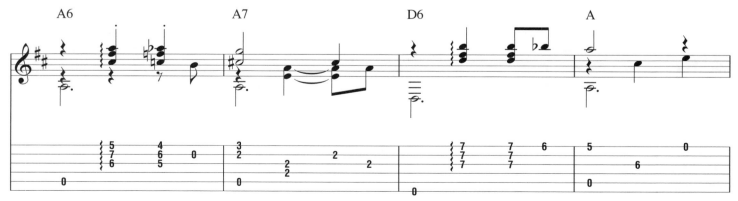

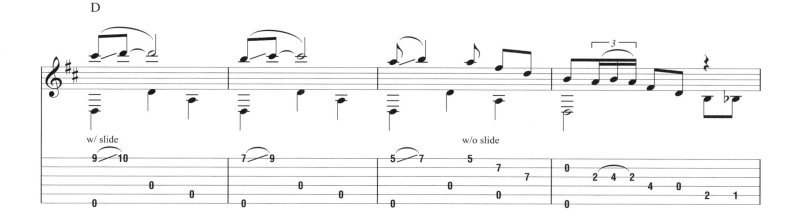

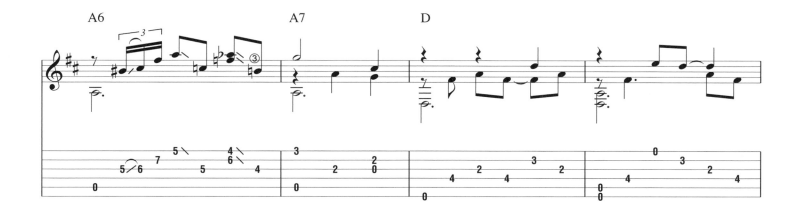

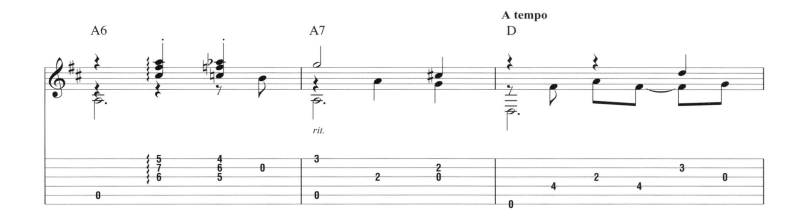

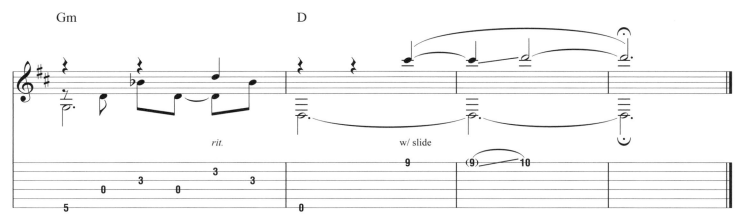

from *Freewayman*

Drivin' Blues

By Pat Donohue

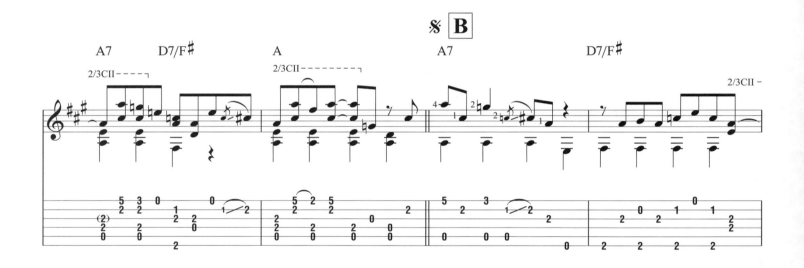

*Chord symbols reflect basic harmony.

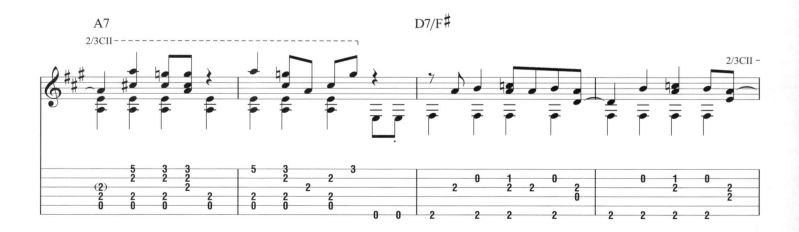

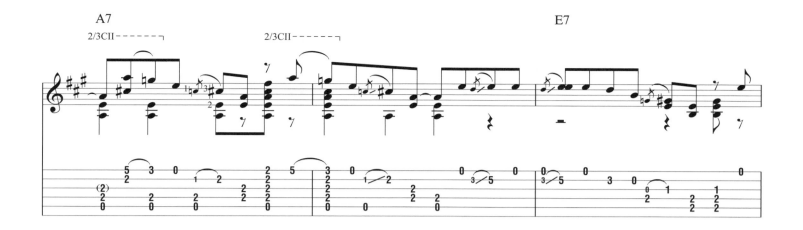

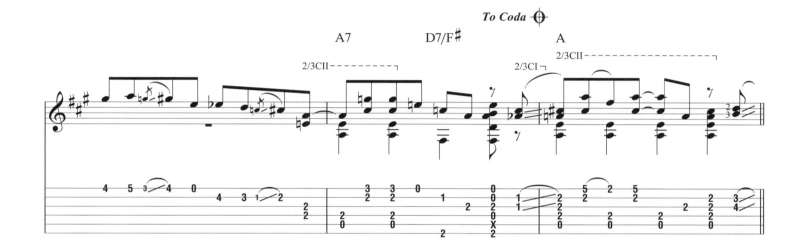

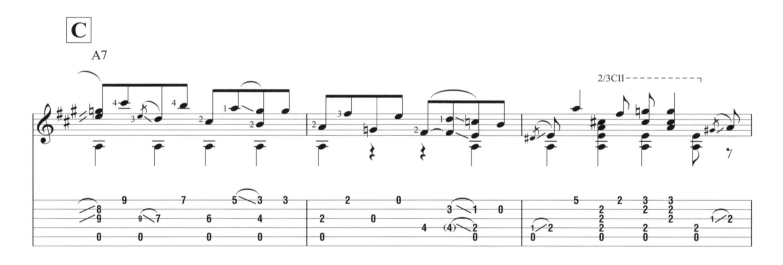

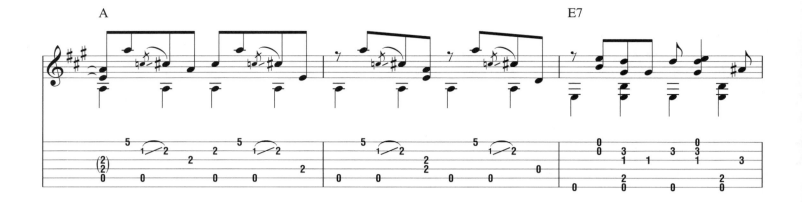

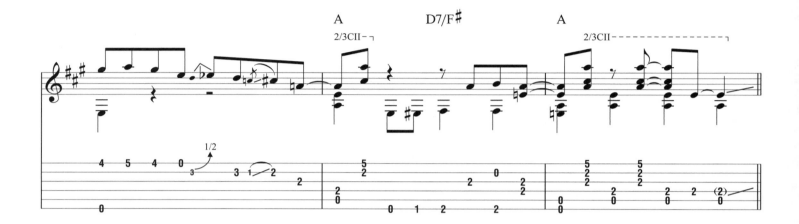

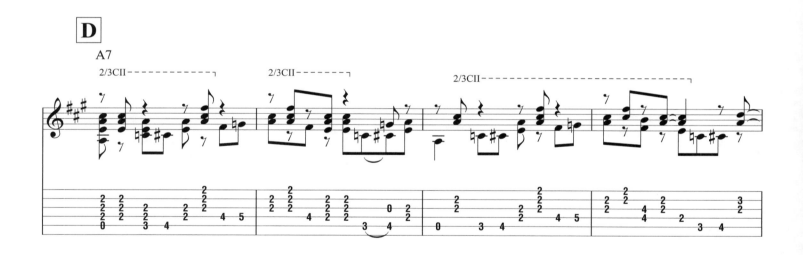

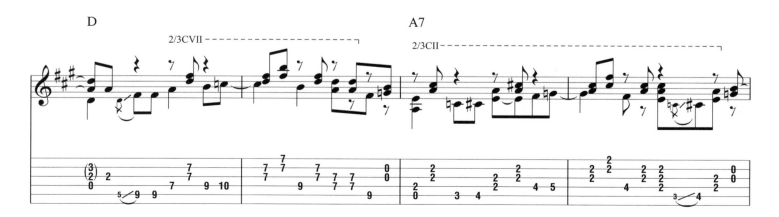

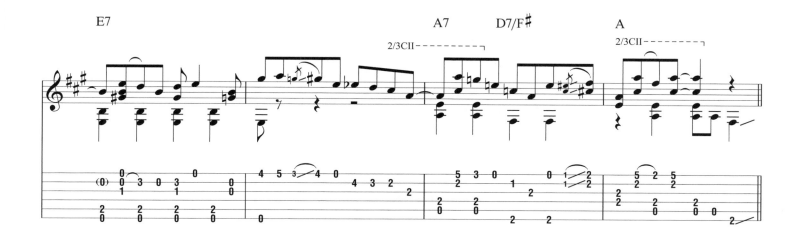

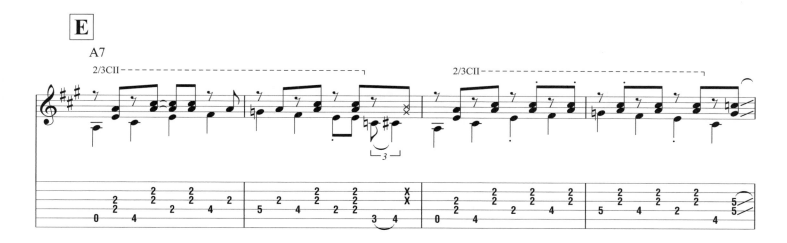

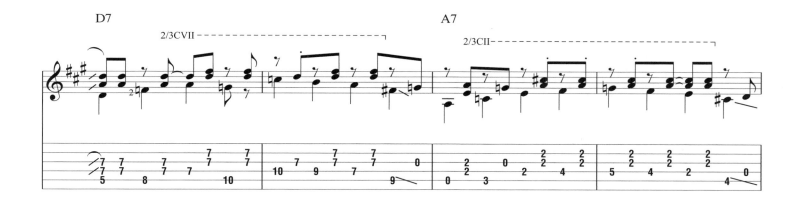

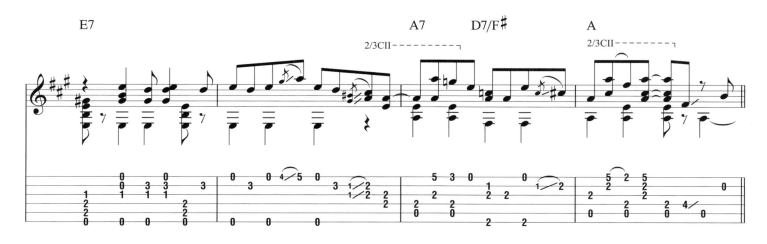

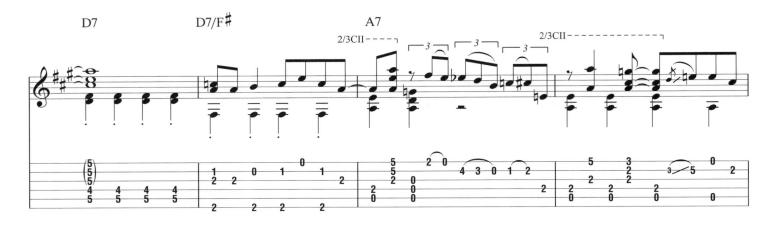

Freewayman

By Pat Donohue

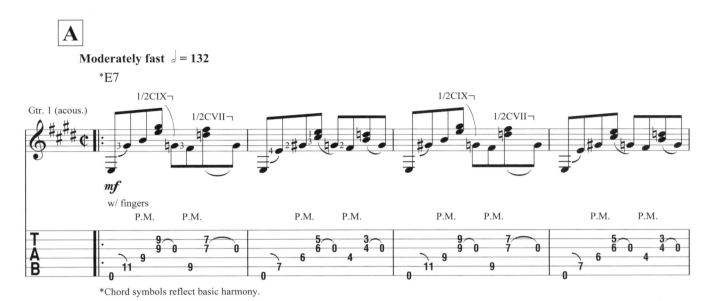

*Chord symbols reflect basic harmony.

4th time, To Coda ⊕

**T = Thumb on 6th string

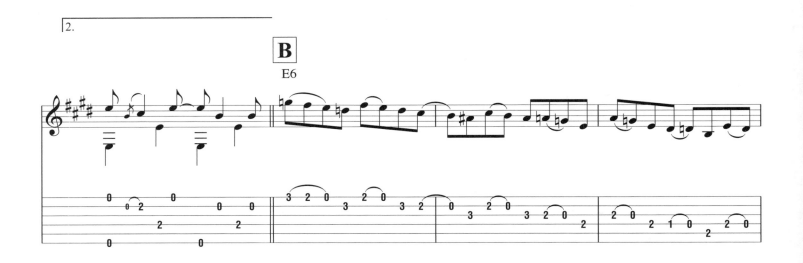

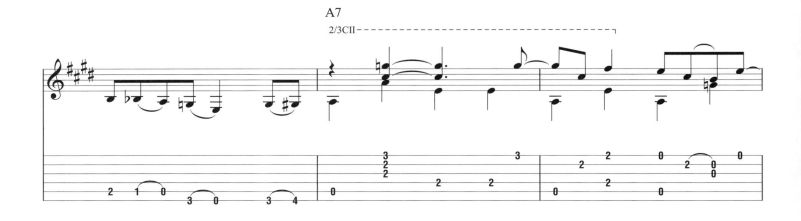

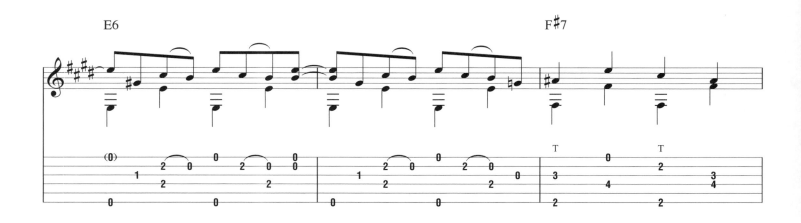

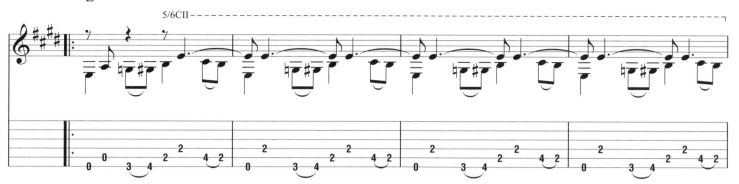

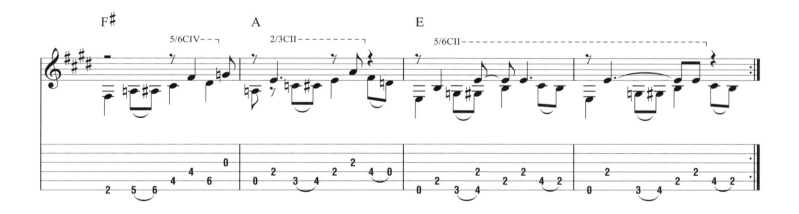

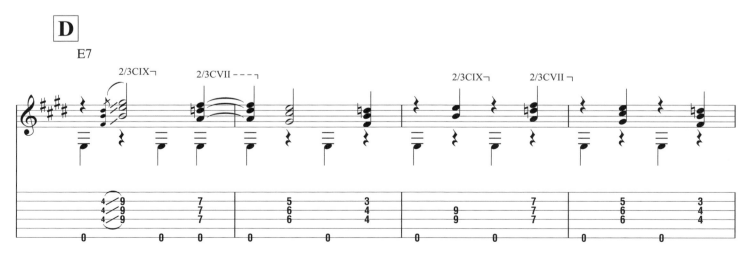

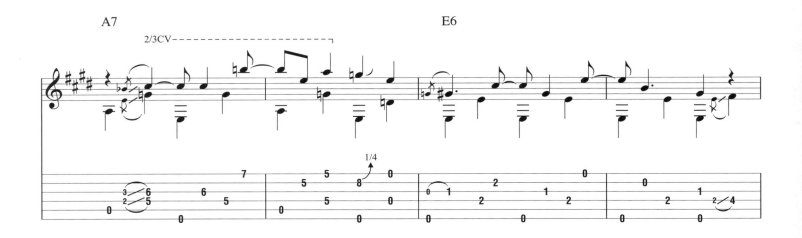

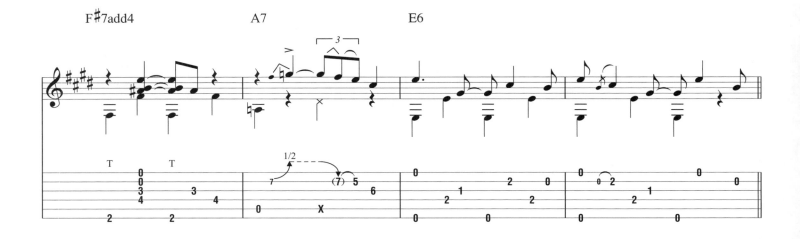

 E

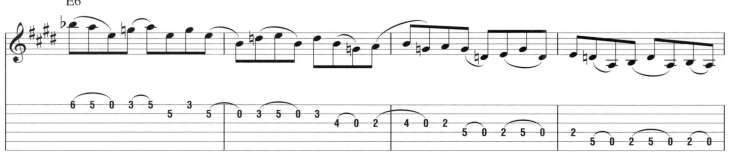

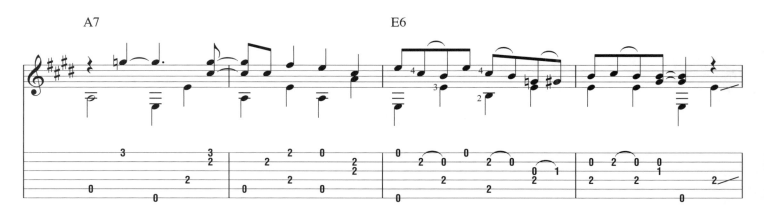

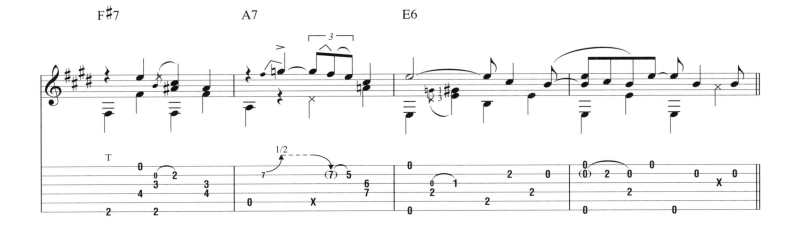

F

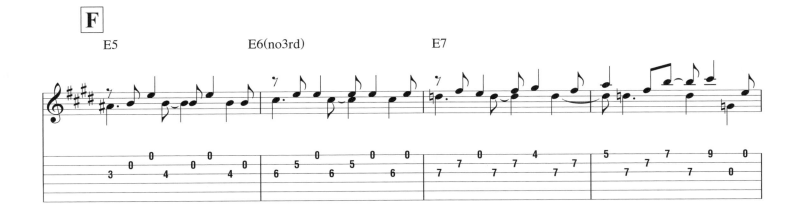

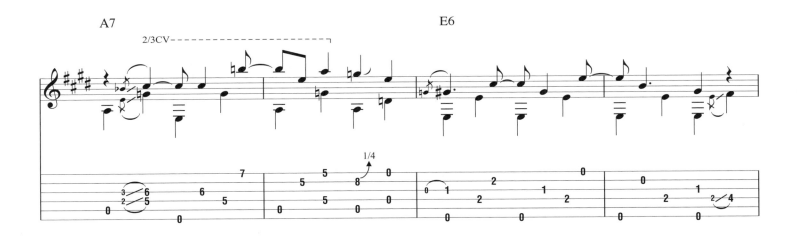

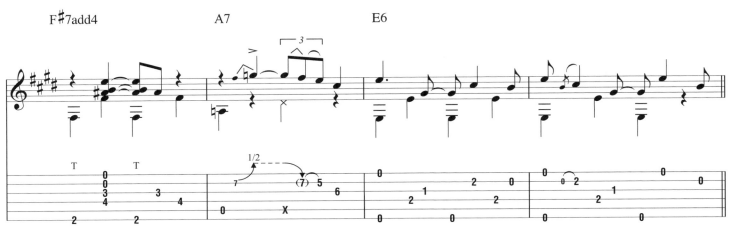

G

E7

A7

E6   F#7add4

D.C. al Coda
(take 1st ending)

A7   E6

⊕ Coda

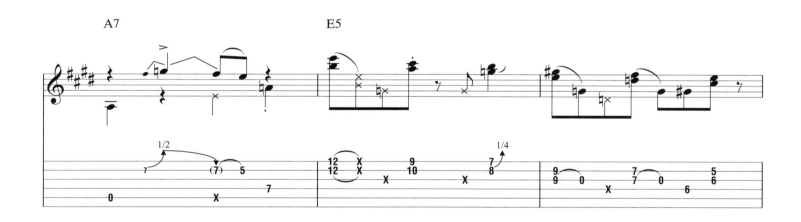

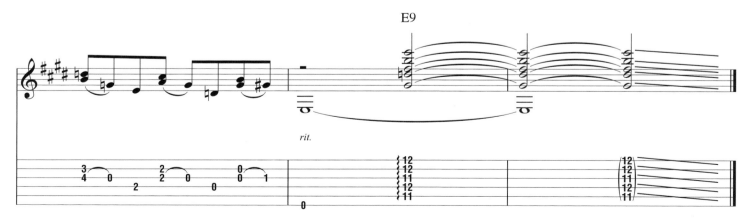

from *American Guitar*

Into the Garden

By Pat Donohue

A

Moderately slow ♩ = 97

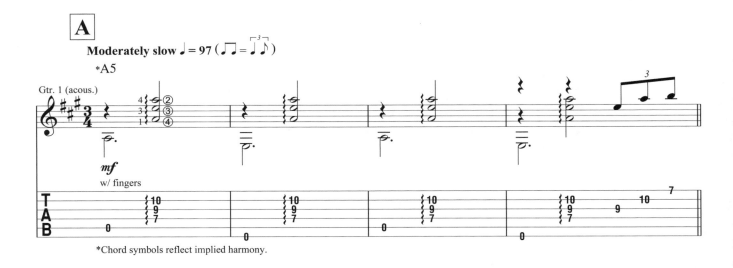

*Chord symbols reflect implied harmony.

B

**T = Thumb on the 6th string

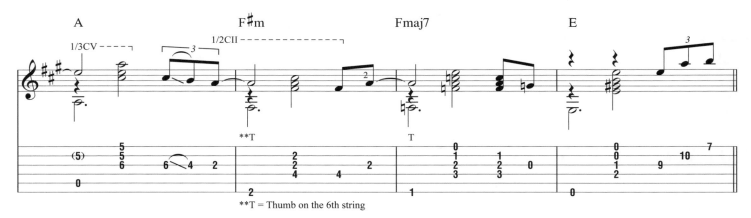

C

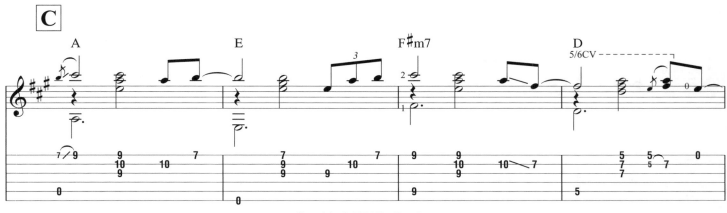

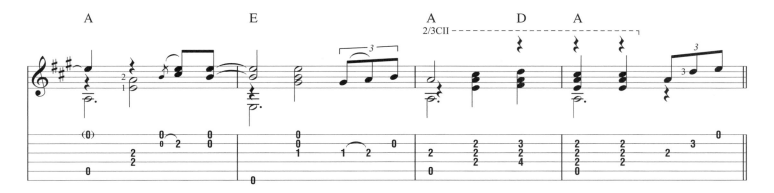

D

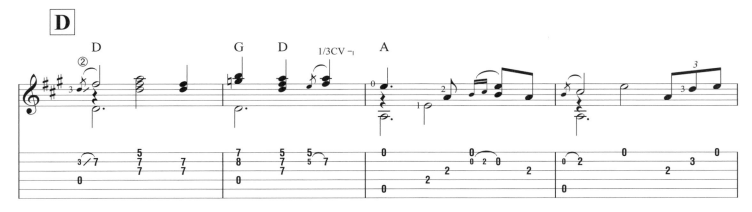

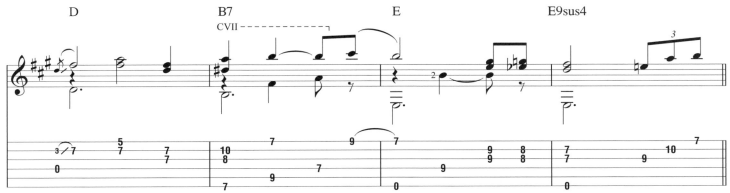

E

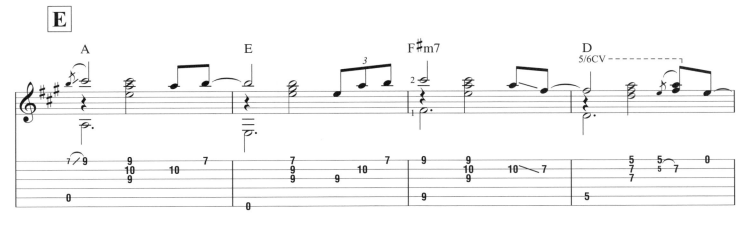

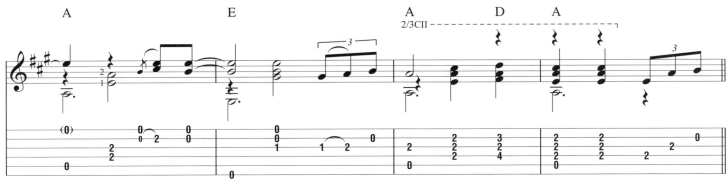

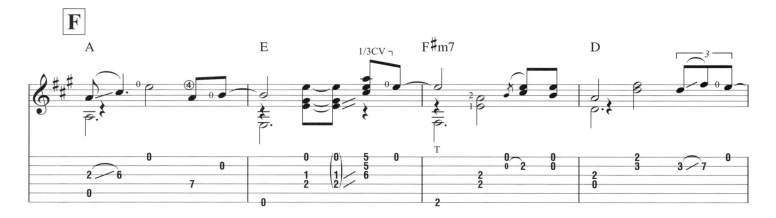

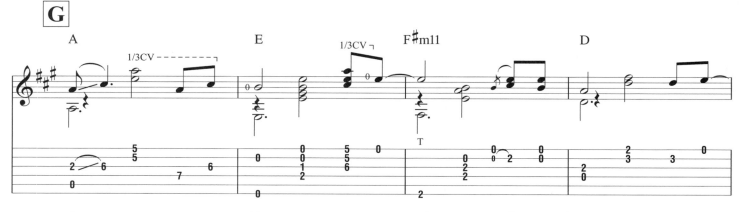

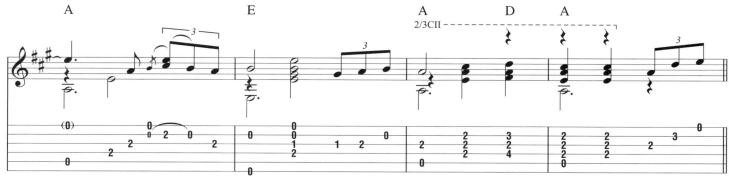

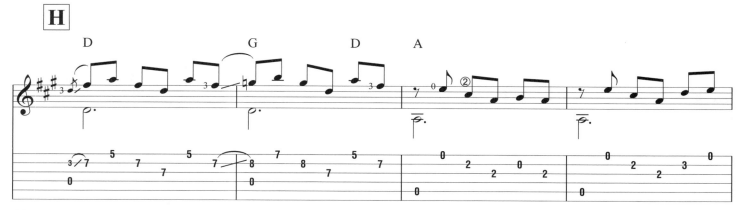

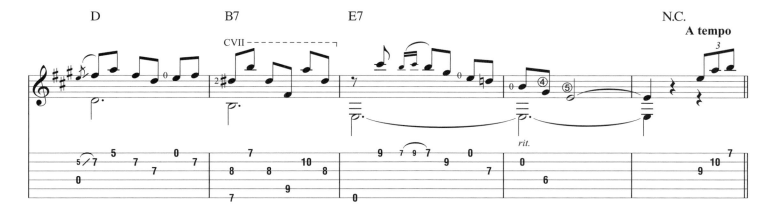

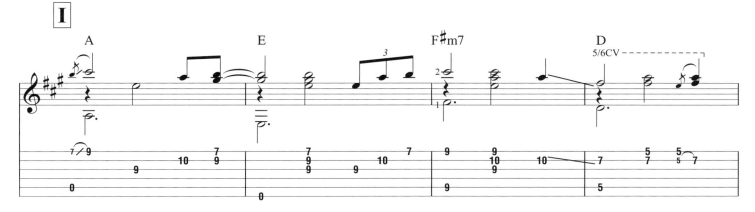

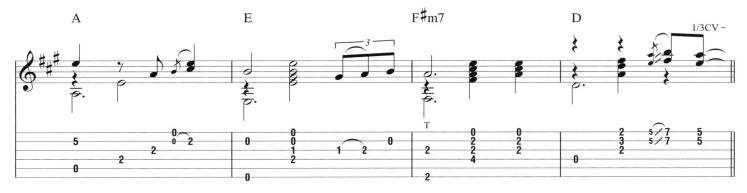

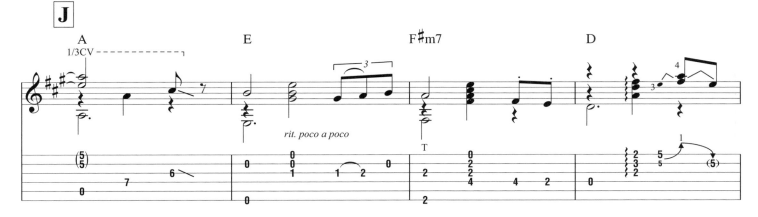

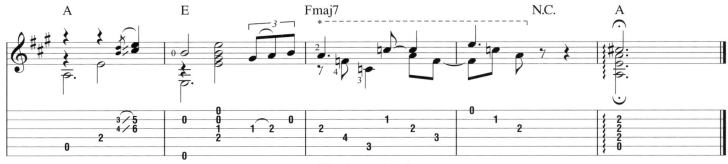

*Played as even eighth-notes.

from *American Guitar*

Joe Fingers

By Pat Donohue

*Chord symbols reflect basic harmony.

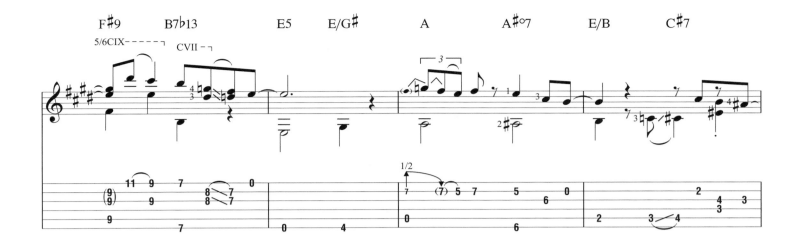

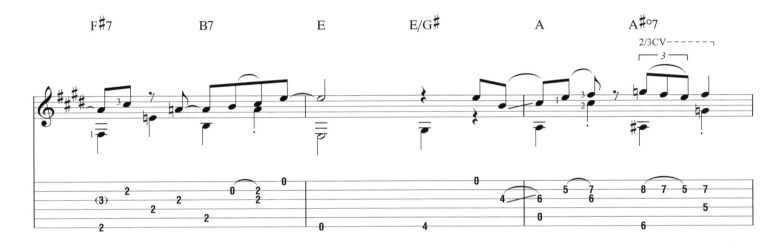

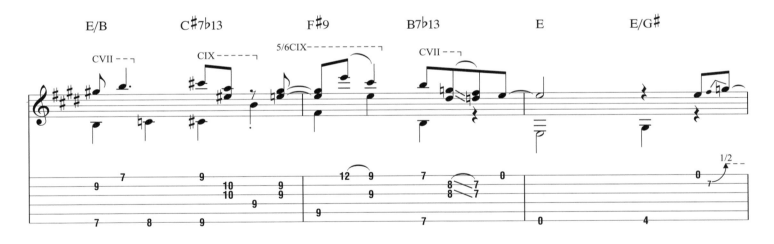

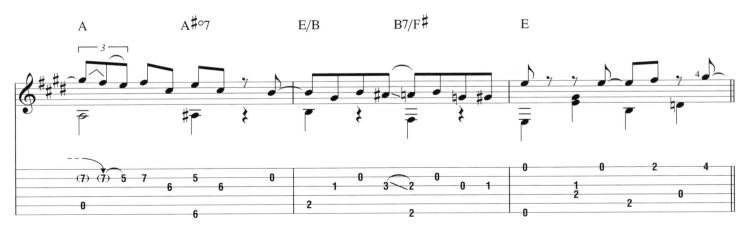

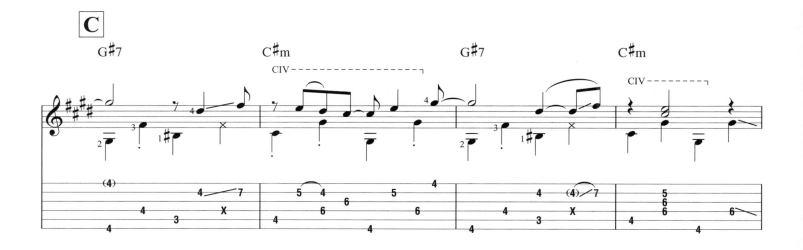

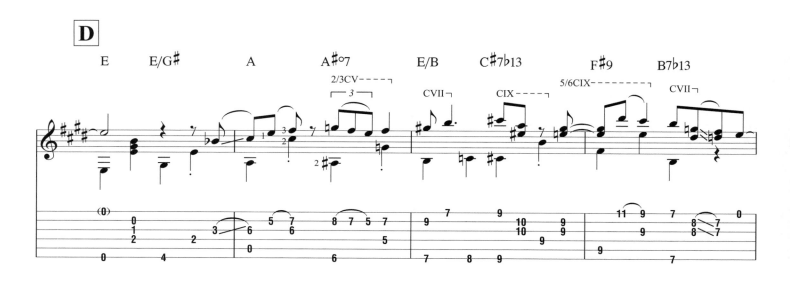

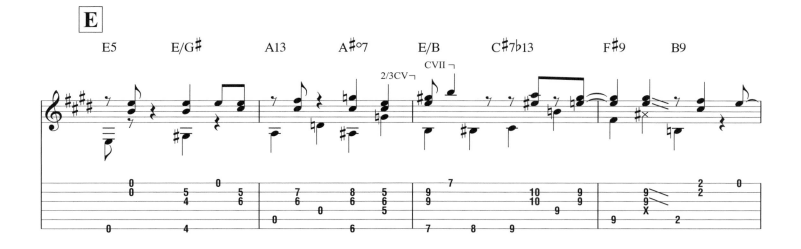

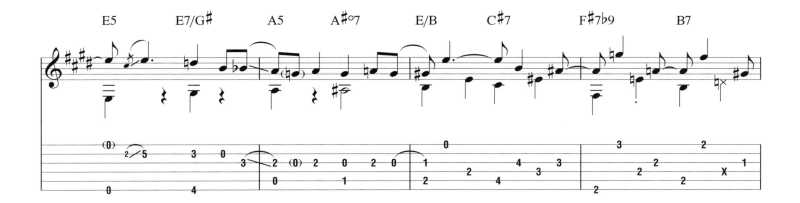

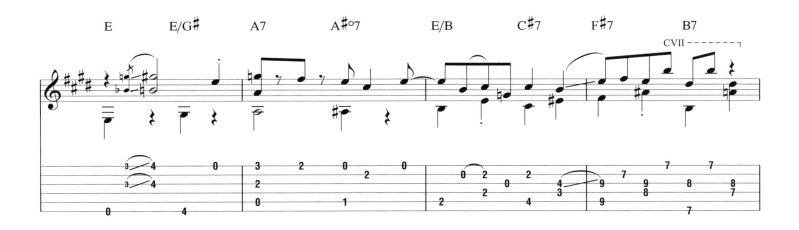

45

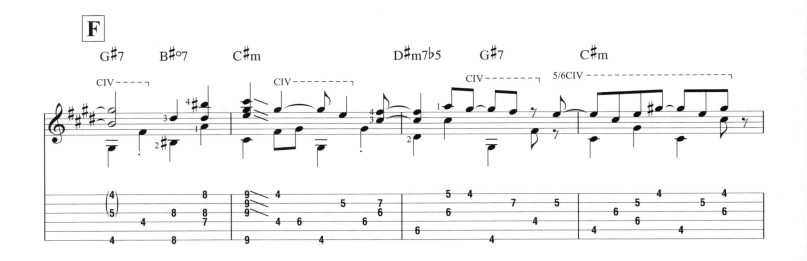

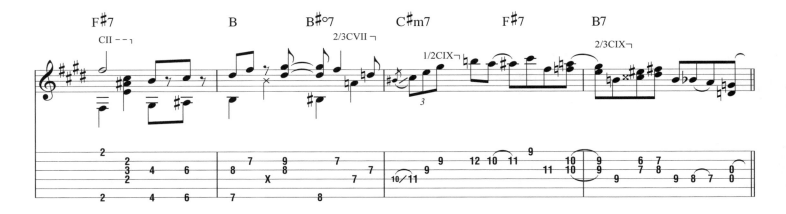

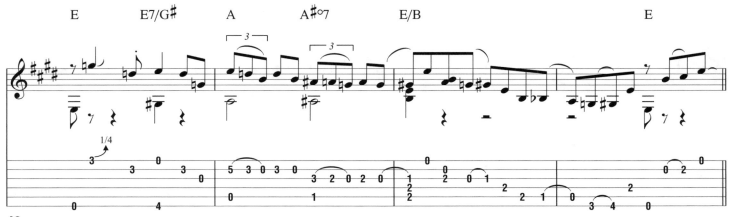

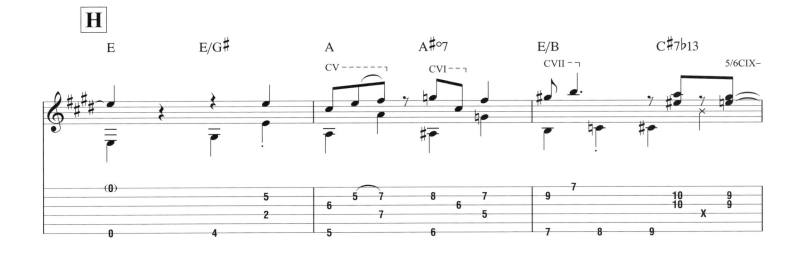

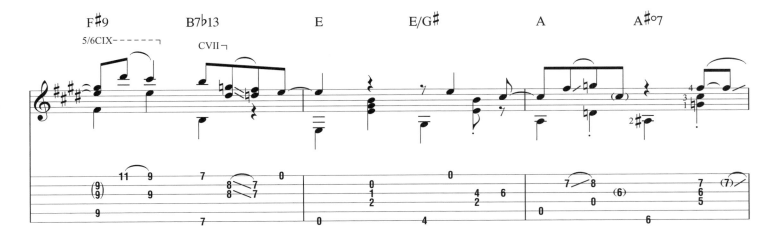

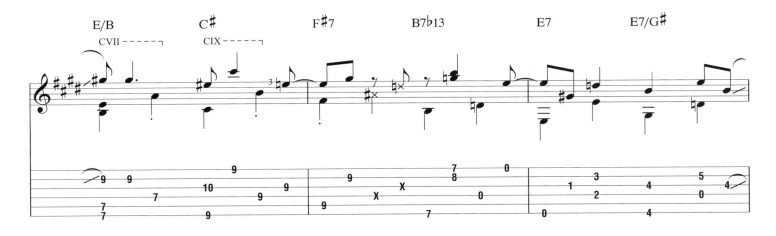

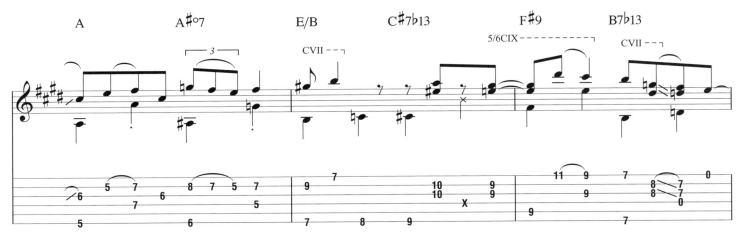

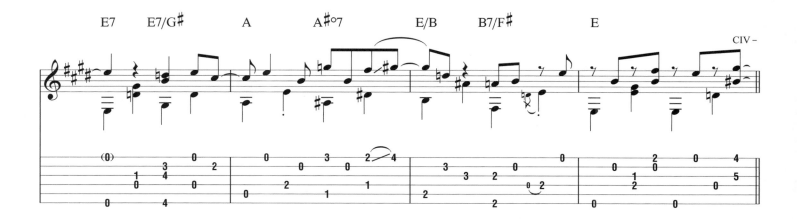

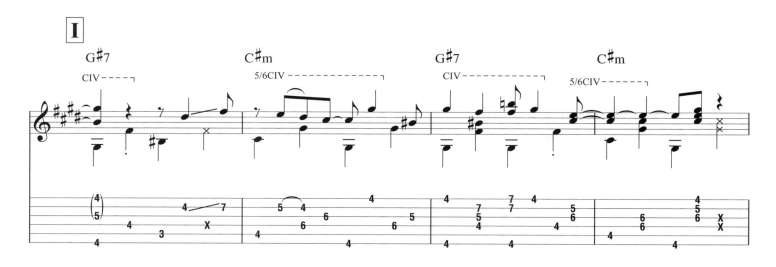

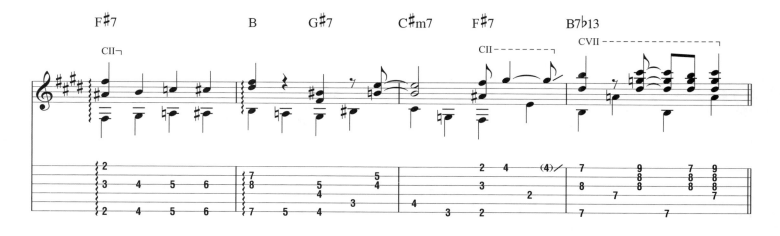

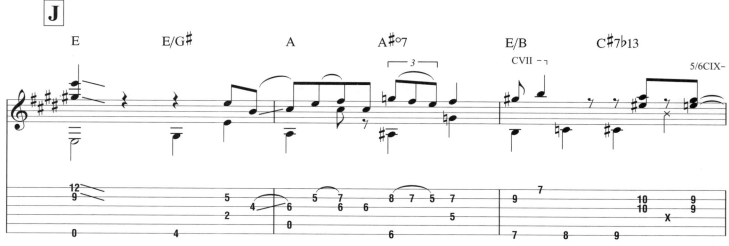

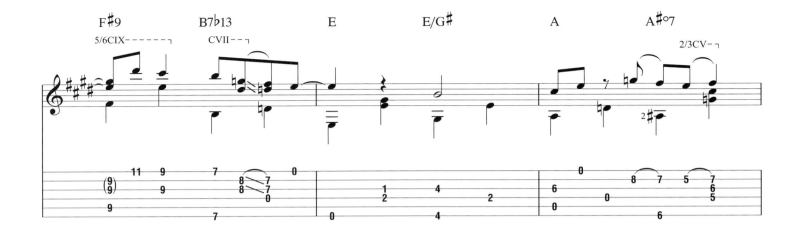

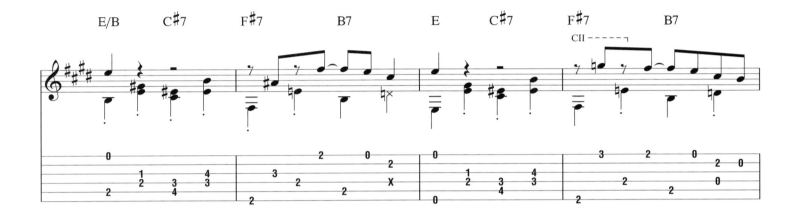

Free time

from *American Guitar*
Maple Leaf Rag

Music by Scott Joplin

*Chord symbols reflect basic harmony.

**T = Thumb on 6th string

*Played as even eighth notes. **Substitute note in parentheses 2nd & 3rd times.

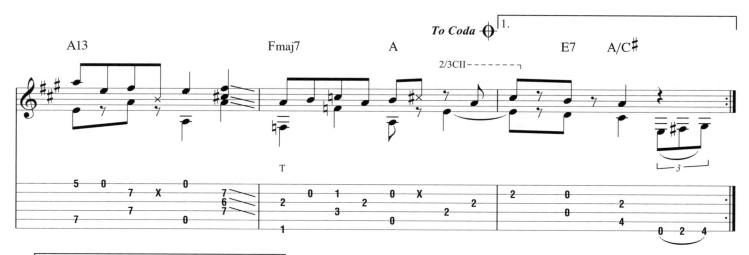

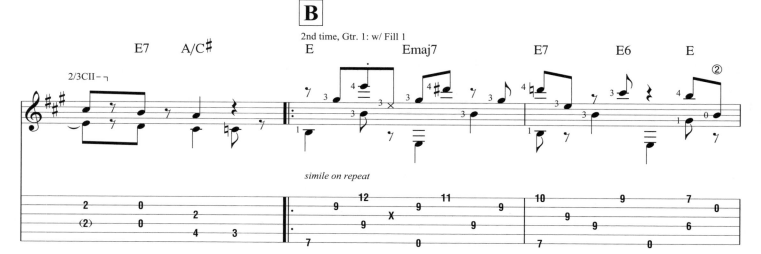

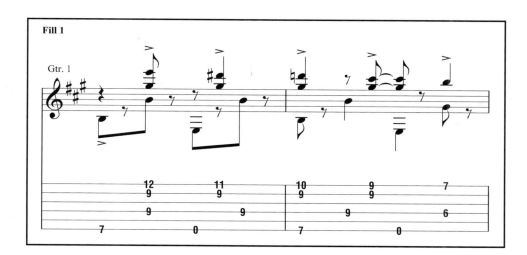

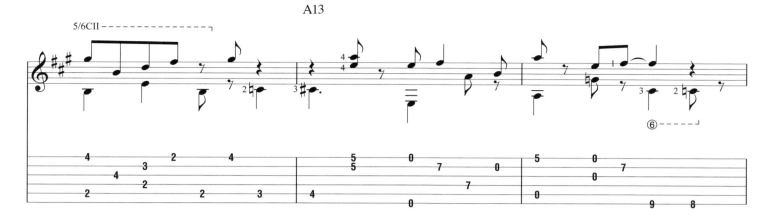

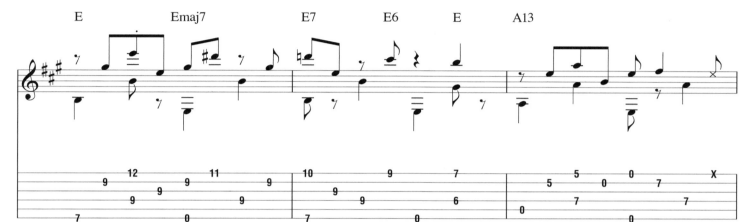

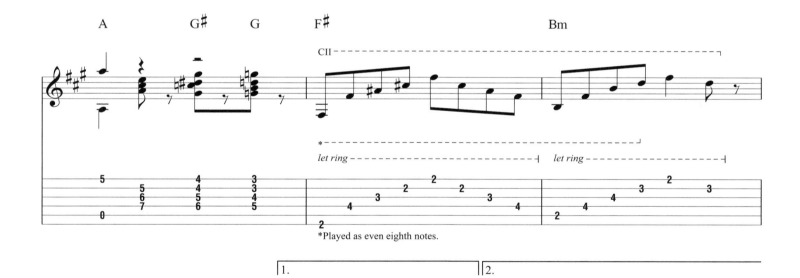

*Played as even eighth notes.

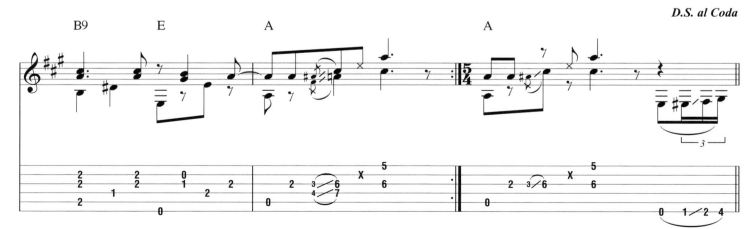

⊕ **Coda**

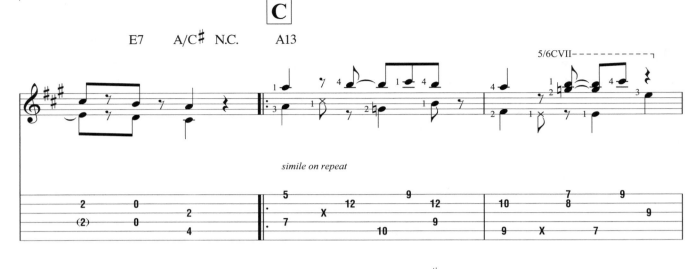

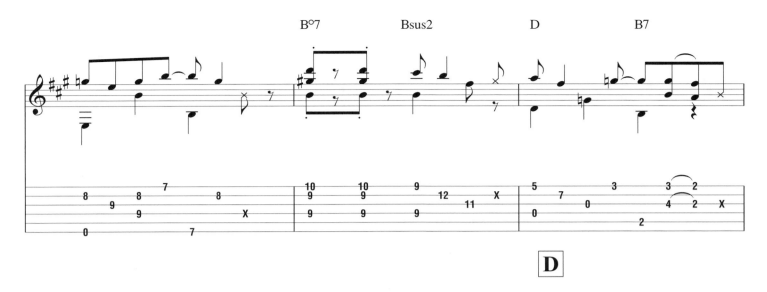

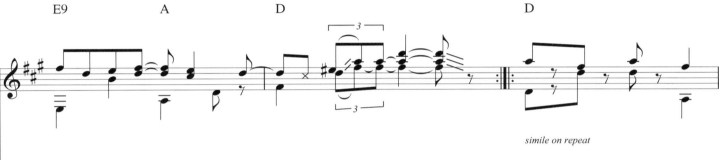

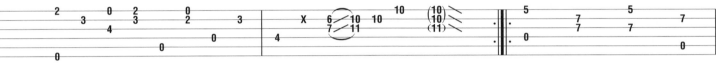

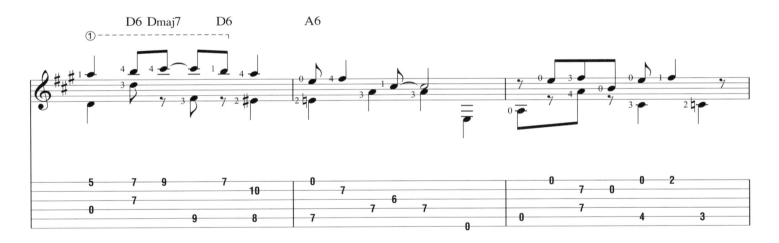

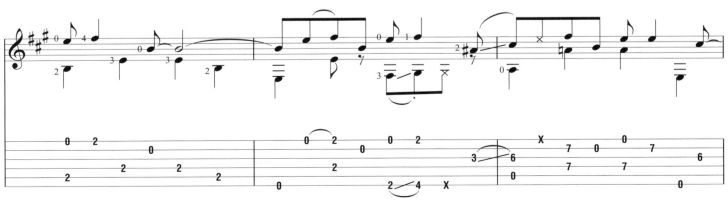

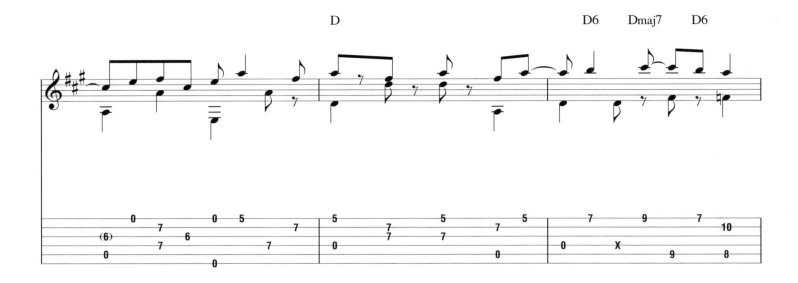

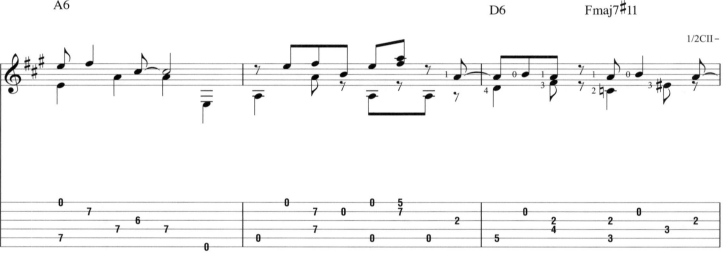

from *Freewayman*

Mountain Air

By Pat Donohue

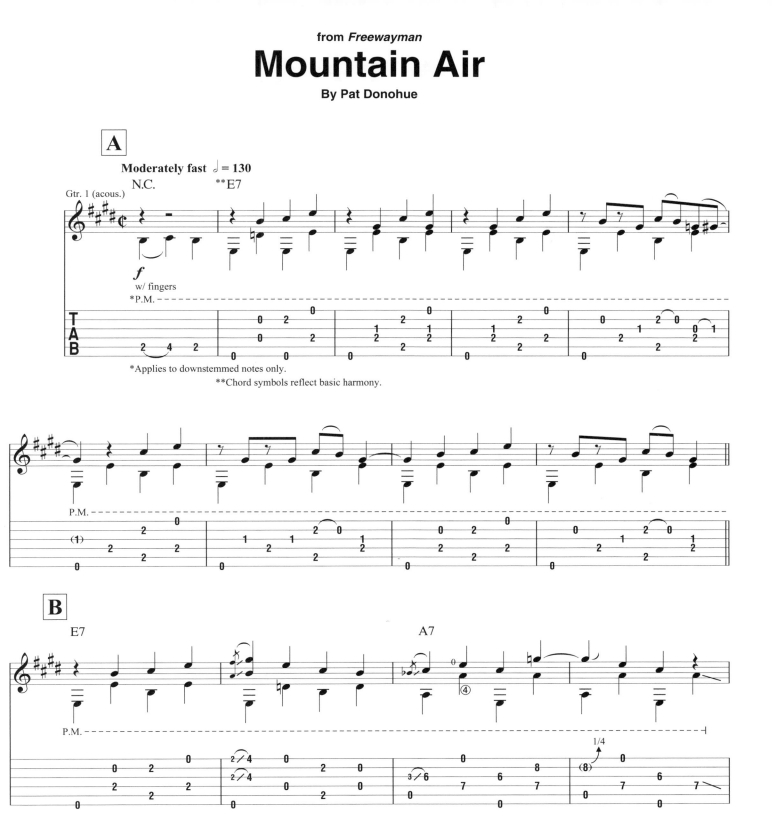

*Applies to downstemmed notes only.
**Chord symbols reflect basic harmony.

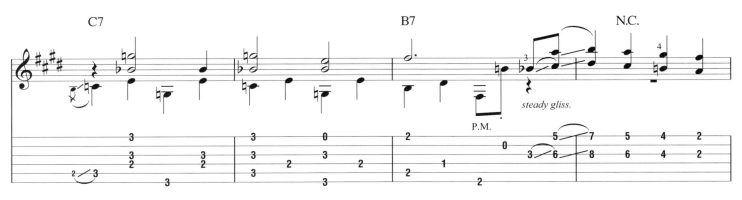

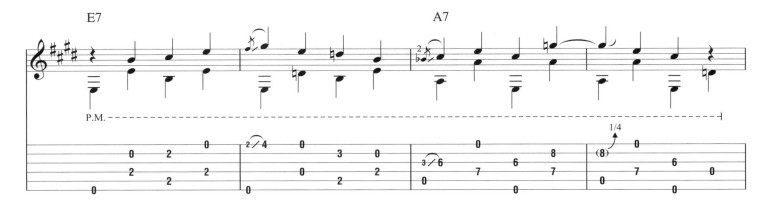

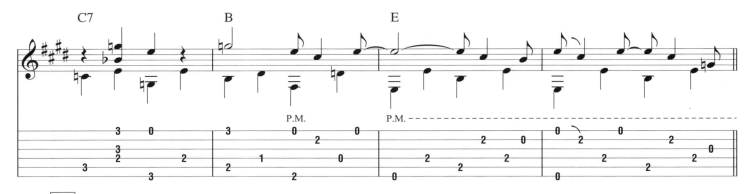

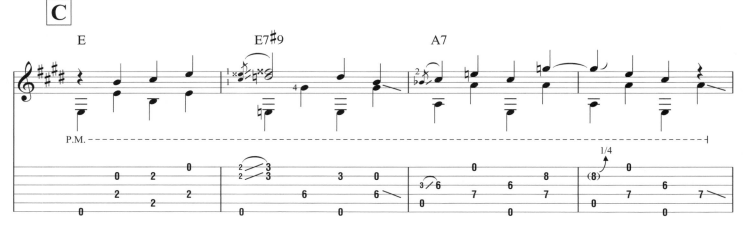

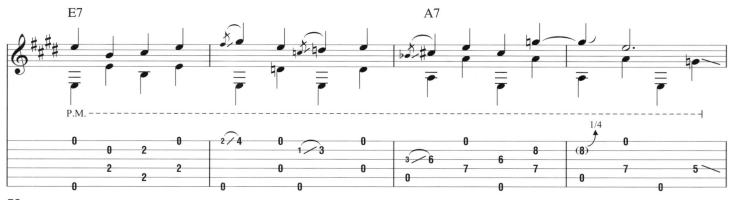

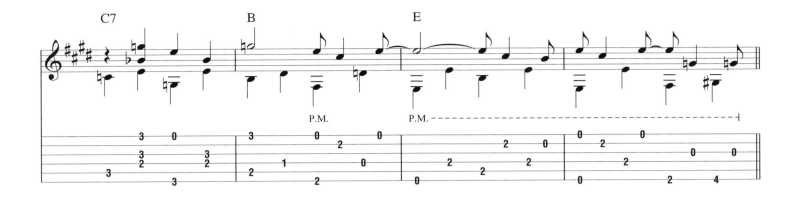

D

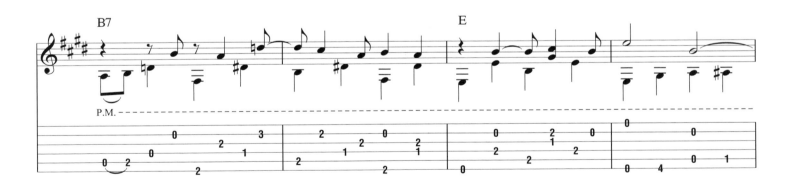

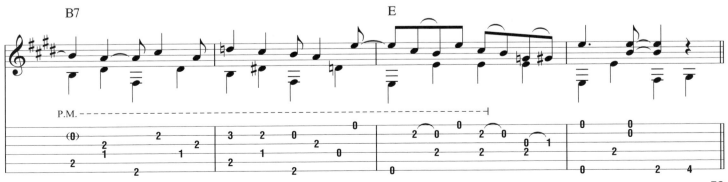

E

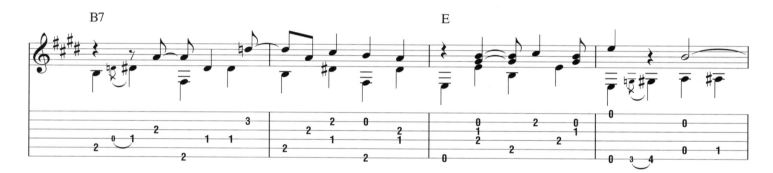

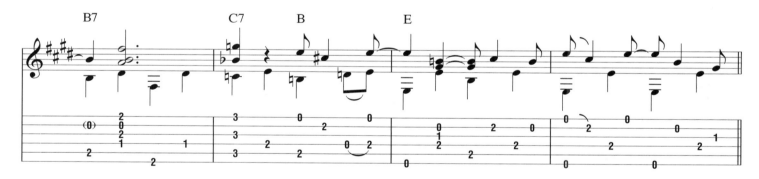

F

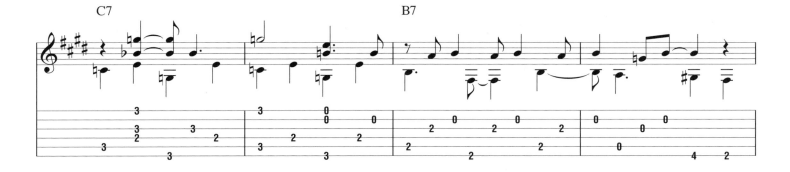

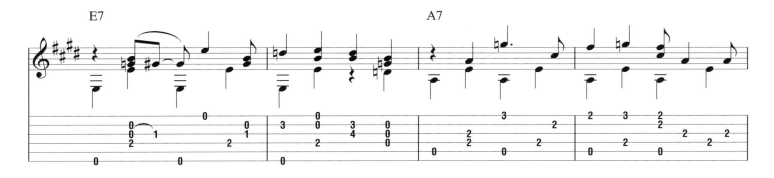

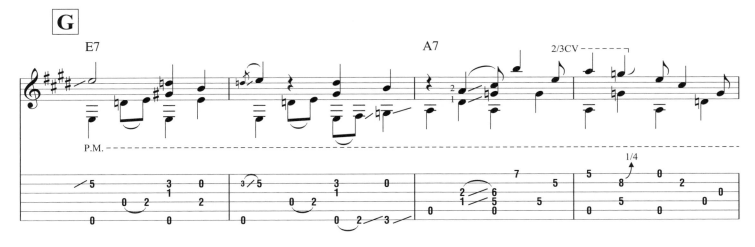

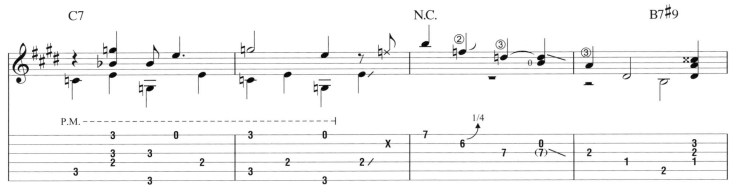

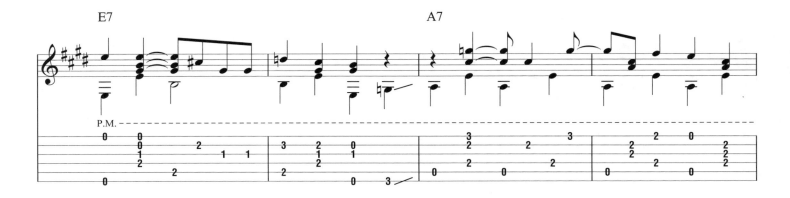

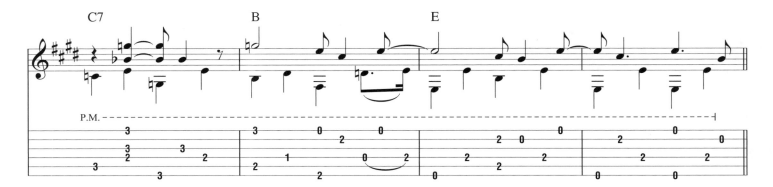

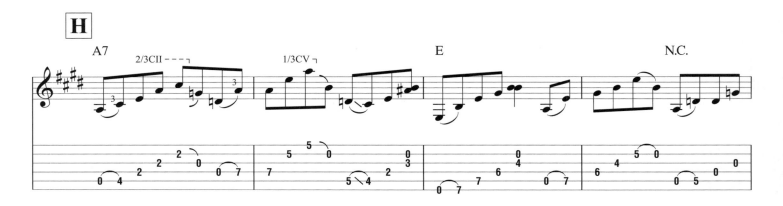

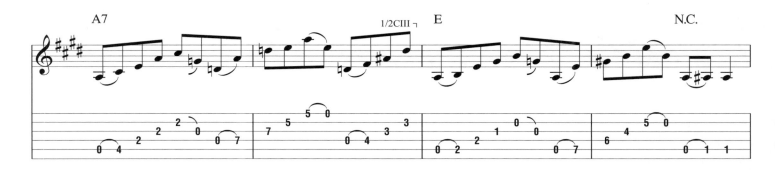

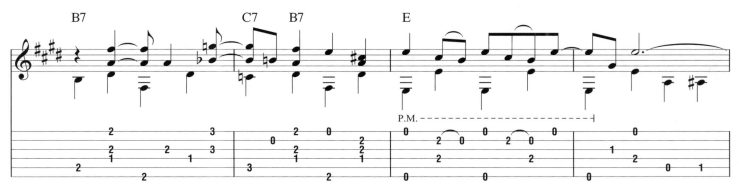

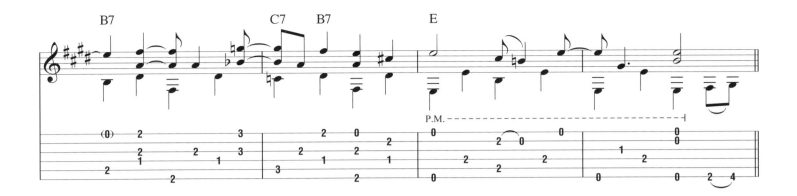

I

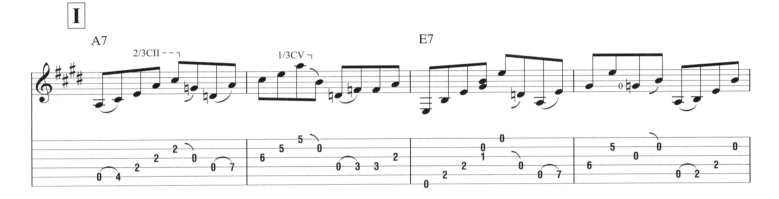

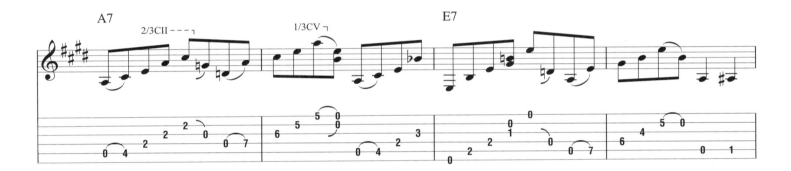

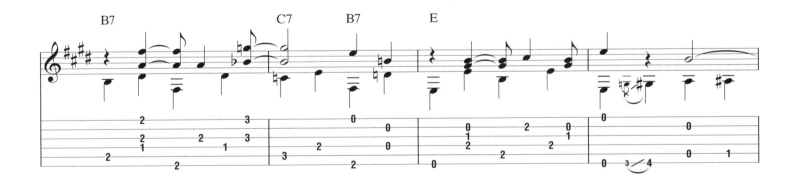

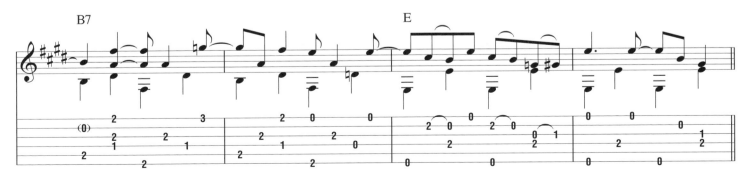

J

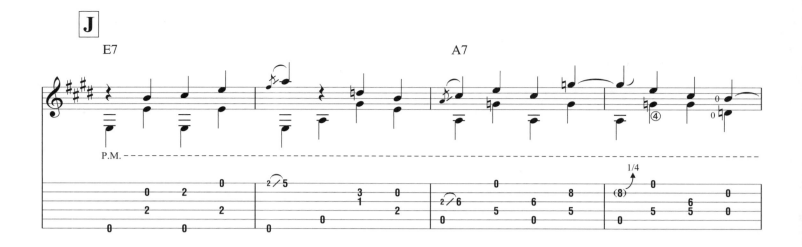

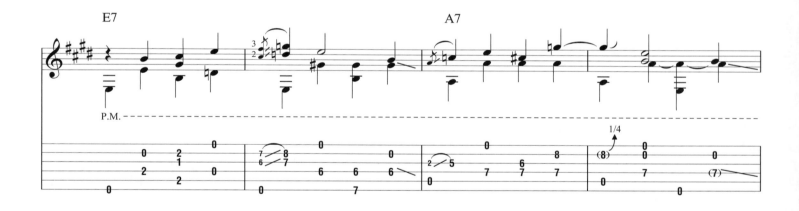

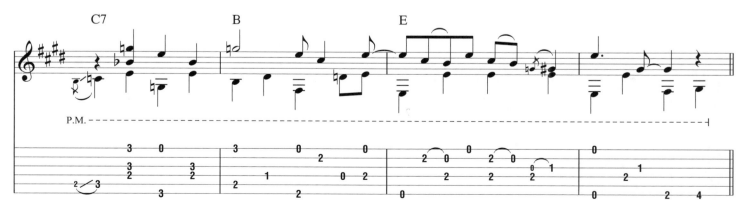

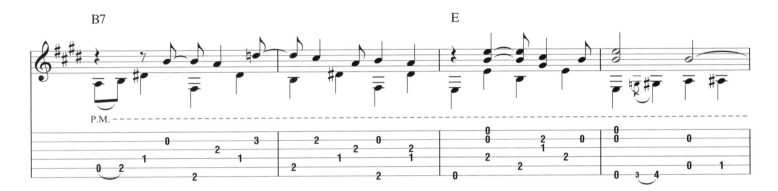

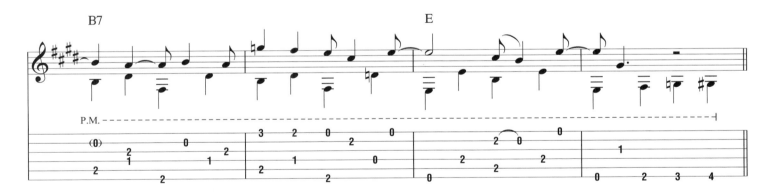

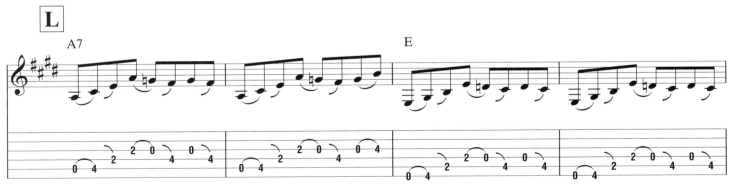

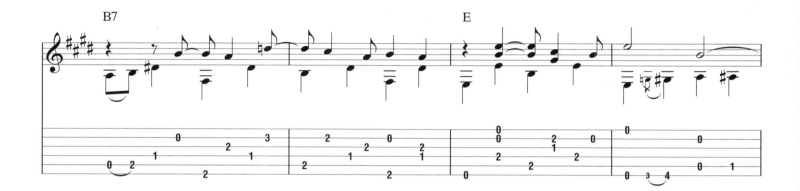

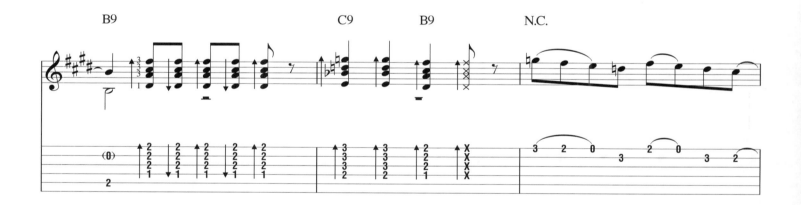

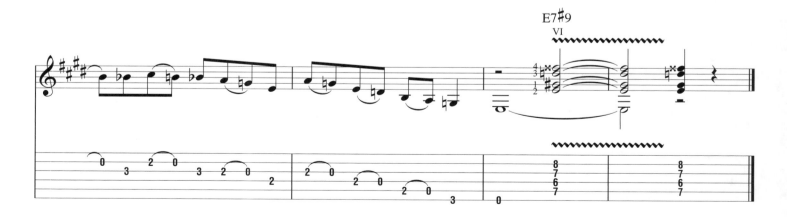

Mudslide

By Pat Donohue

Gtr. 1: Open D tuning:
(low to high) D-A-D-F♯-A-D

*Chord symbols reflect basic harmony.
**P.M. 6th - 3rd strings only.

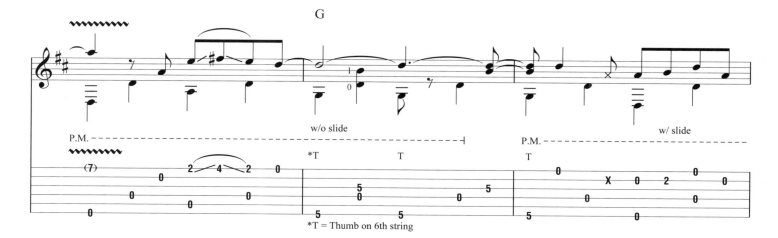

G

w/o slide

w/ slide

P.M.

P.M.

*T = Thumb on 6th string

D

steady
gliss.

P.M.

P.M.

P.M.

G

C

Bm

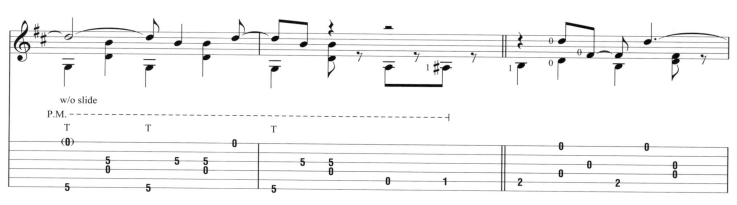

w/o slide

P.M.

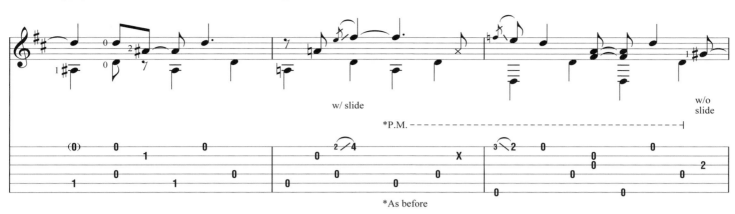

A#+   D

w/ slide   w/o slide

*P.M.

*As before

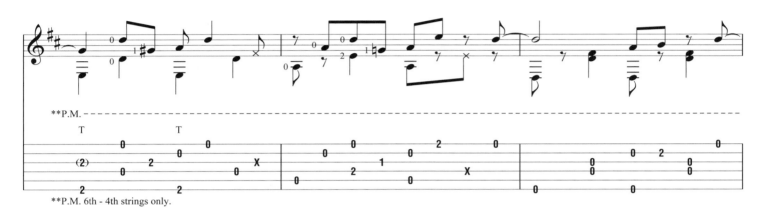

E7add11   A7sus4   D

**P.M.

**P.M. 6th - 4th strings only.

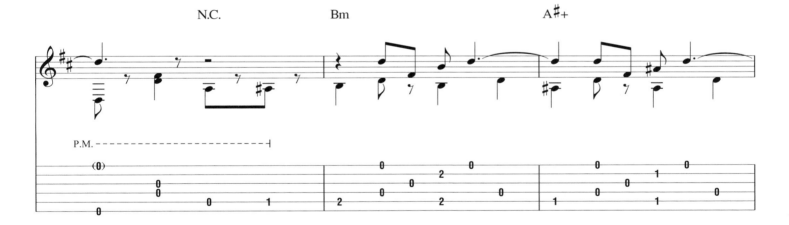

N.C.   Bm   A#+

P.M.

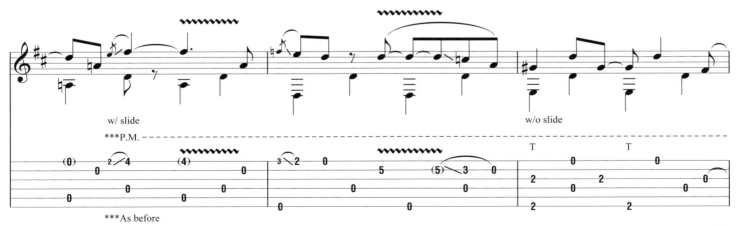

D   E7add11

w/ slide   w/o slide

***P.M.

***As before

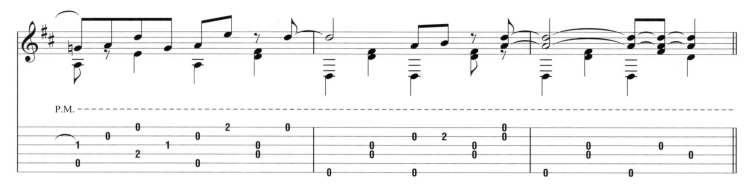

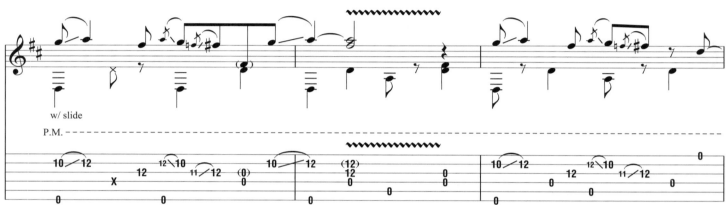

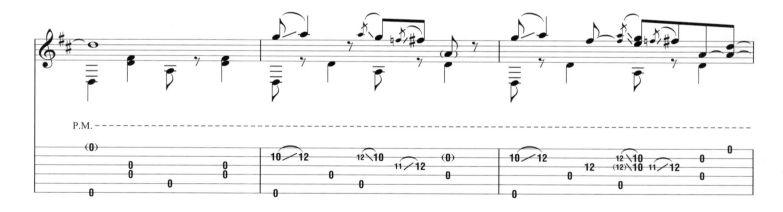

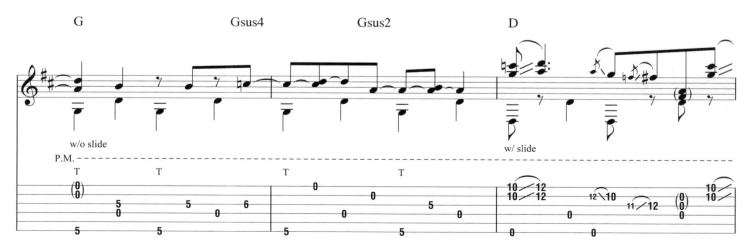

G   Gsus4

E

Bm   A#+

D   E7add11

*As before

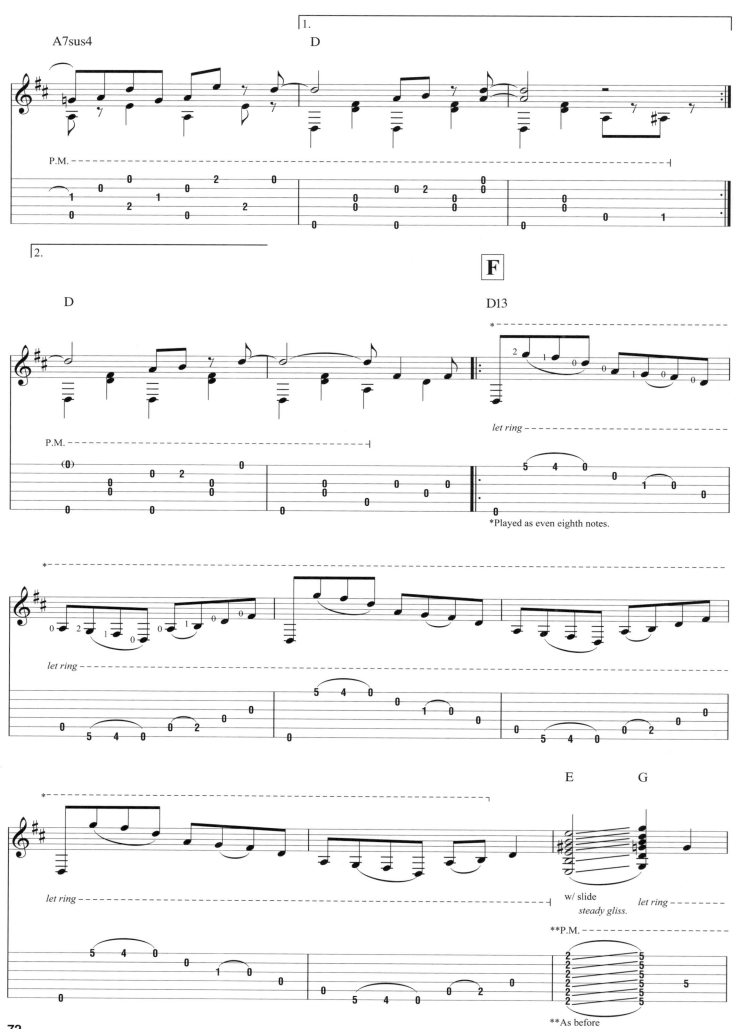

*Played as even eighth notes.

**As before

72

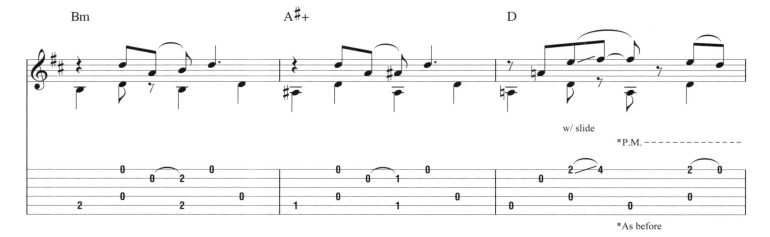

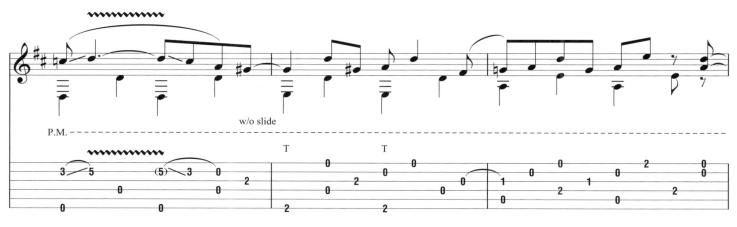

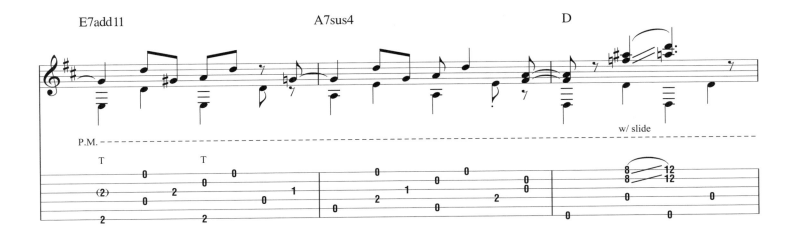

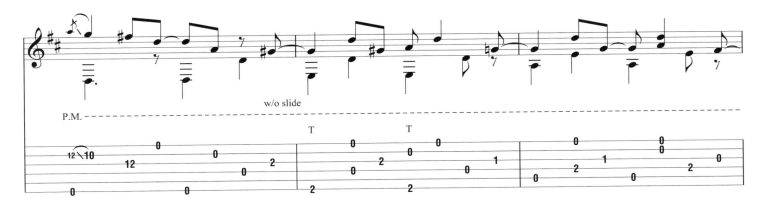

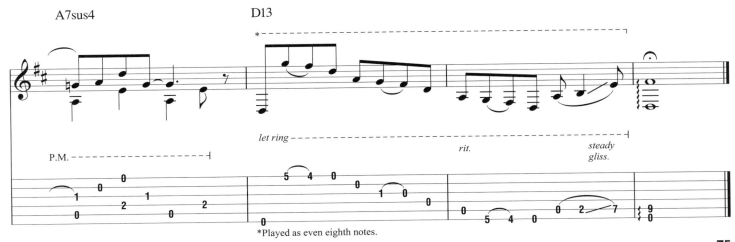

*Played as even eighth notes.

from *American Guitar*

Novocaine

By Pat Donohue

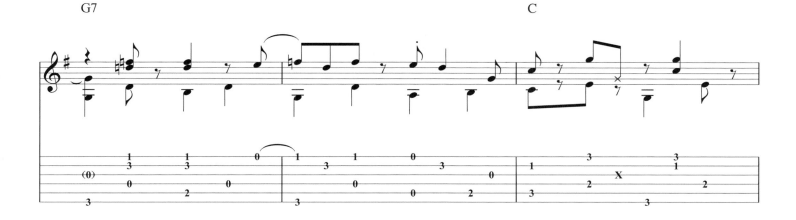

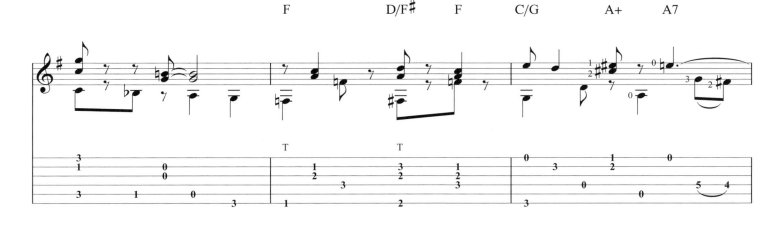

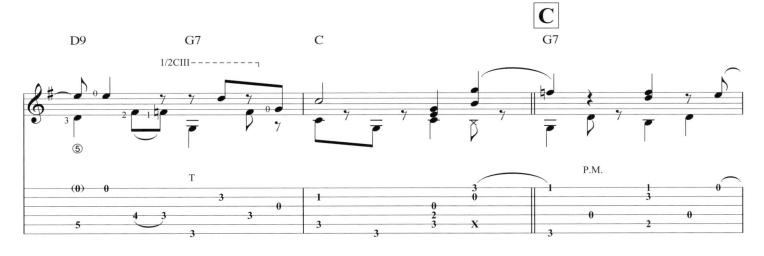

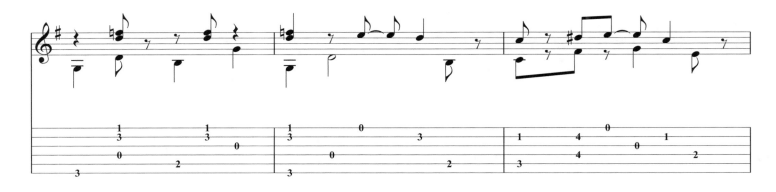

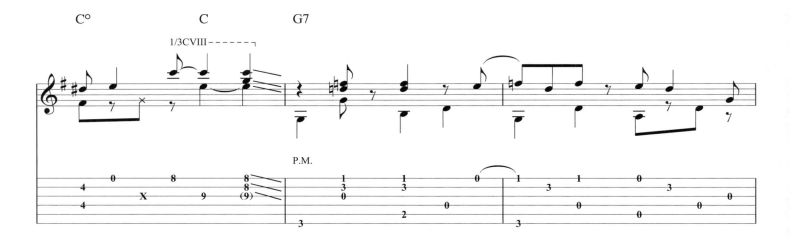

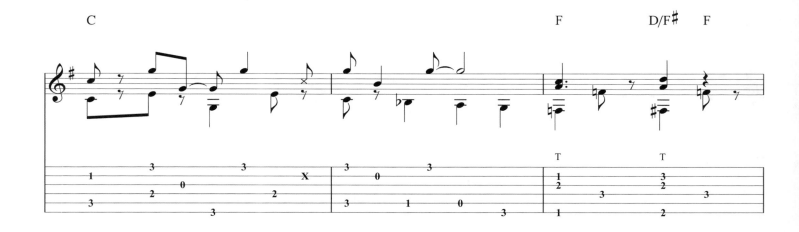

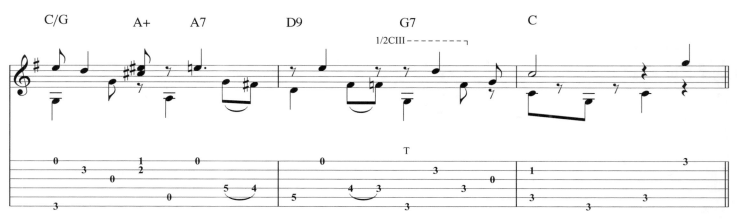

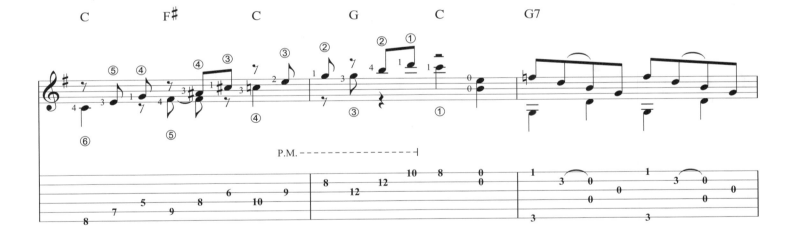

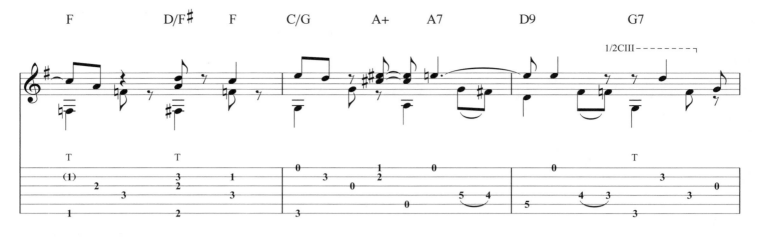

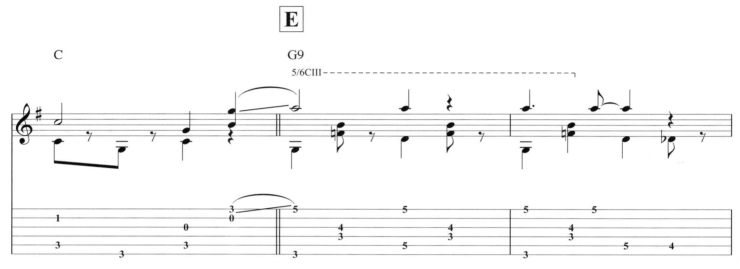

E

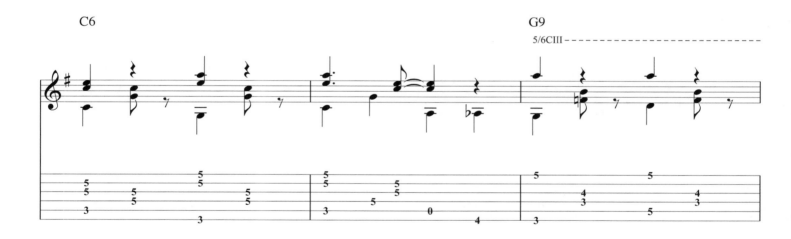

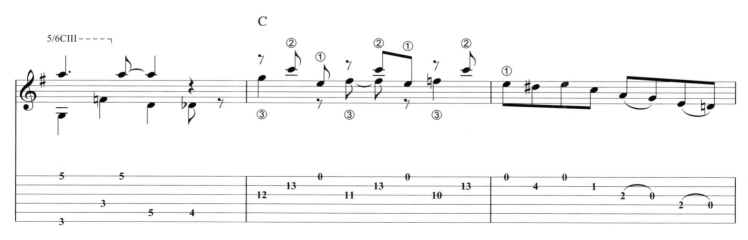

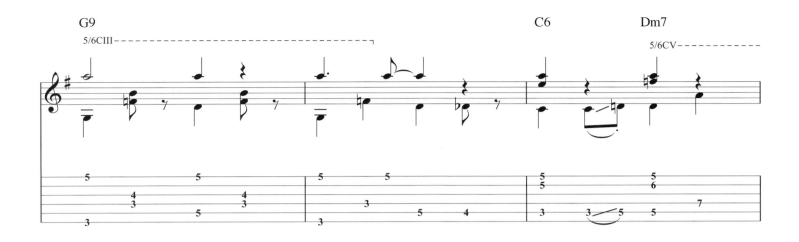

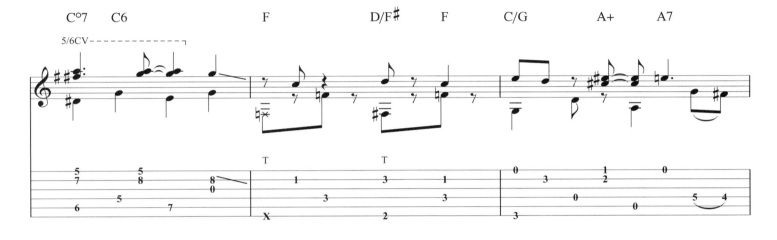

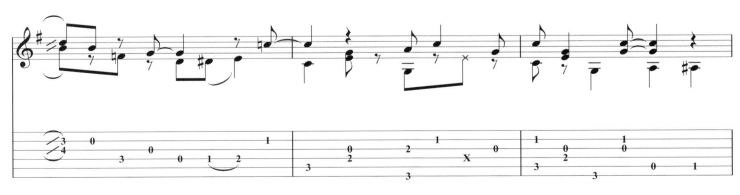

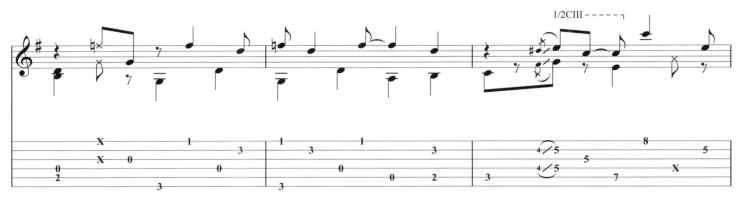

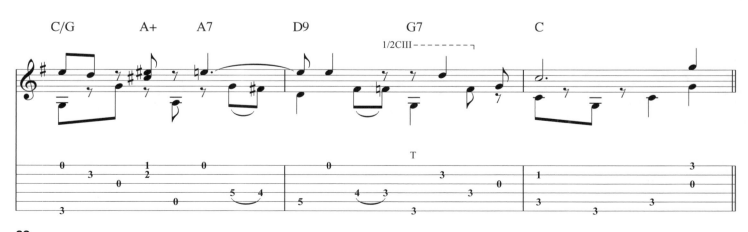

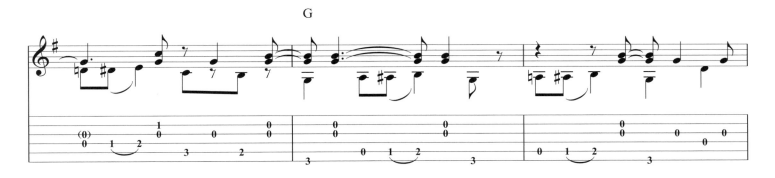

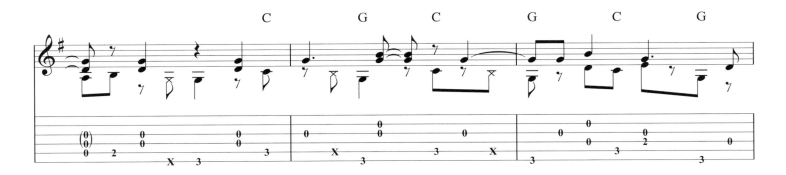

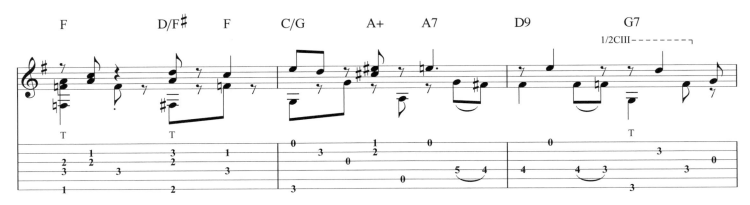

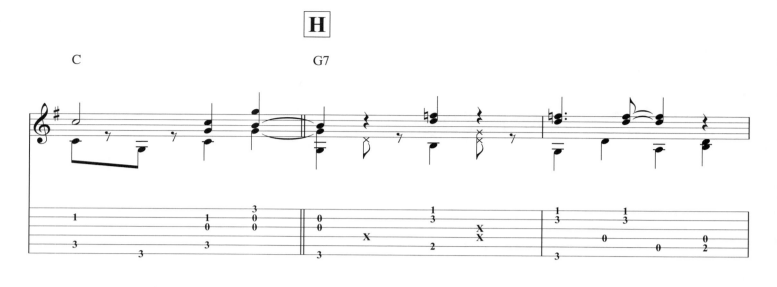

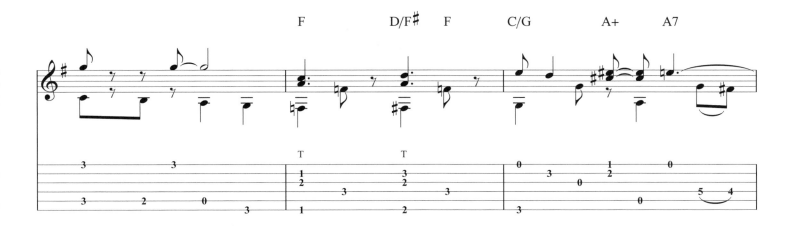

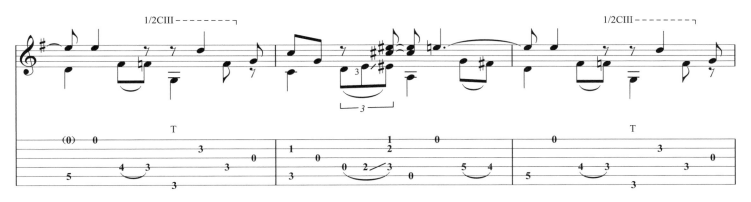

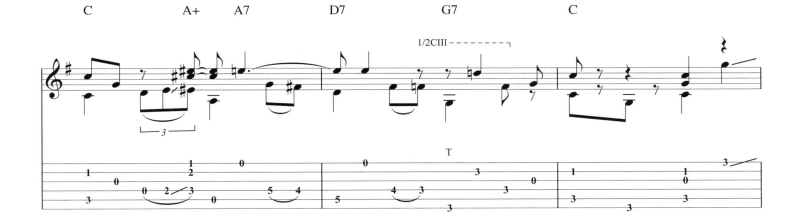

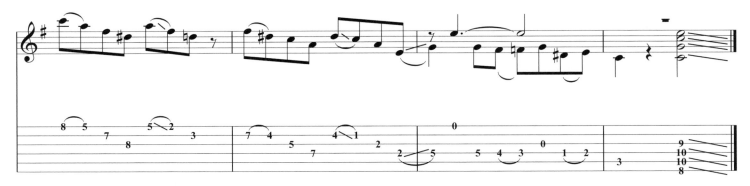

Whole Lotta You

By Pat Donohue

Drop D tuning:
(low to high) D-A-D-G-B-E

*Chord symbols reflect basic harmony.

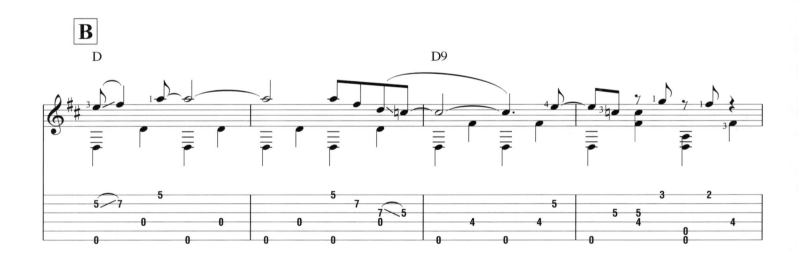

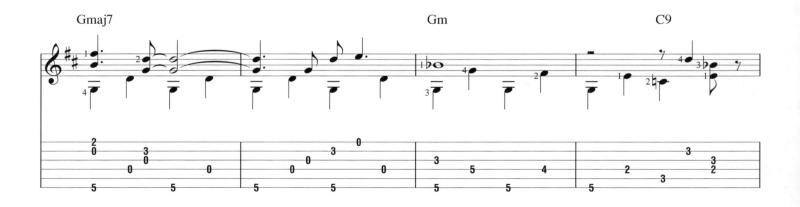

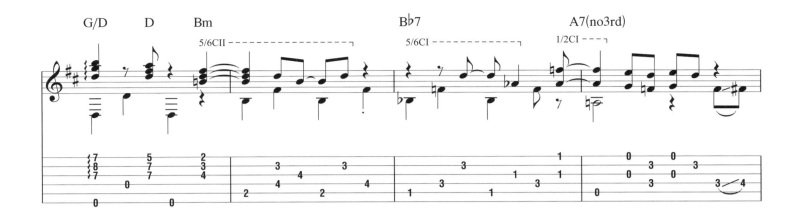

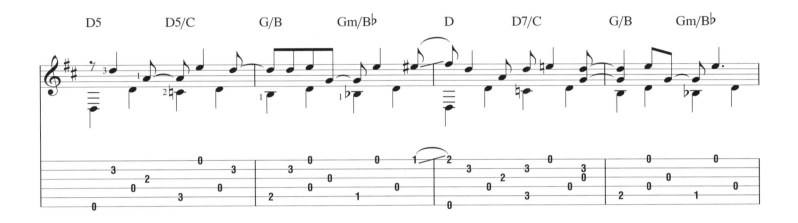

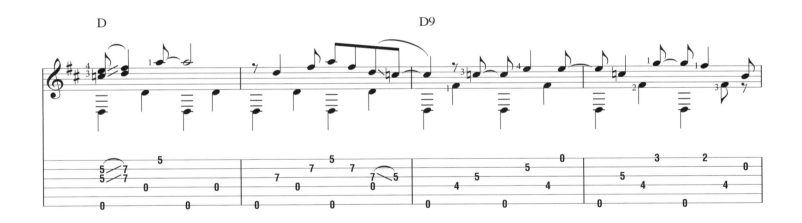

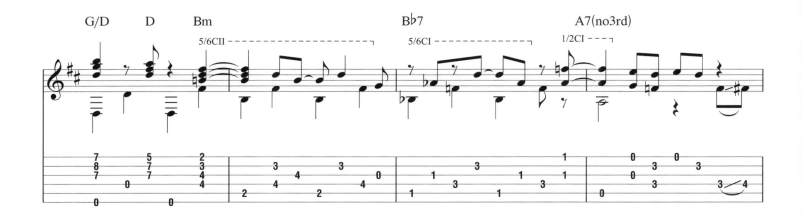

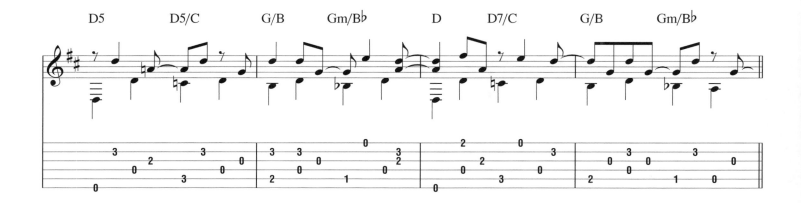

C

*T = Thumb on 6th string

D

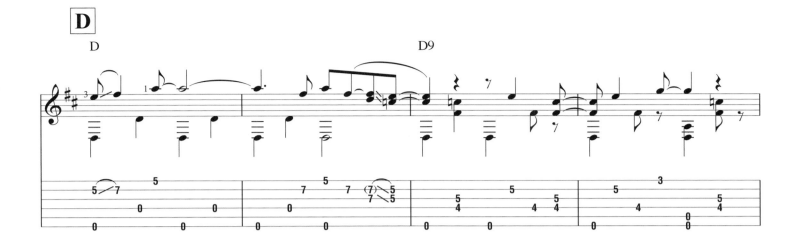

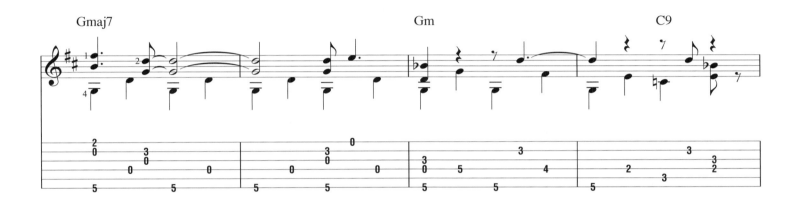

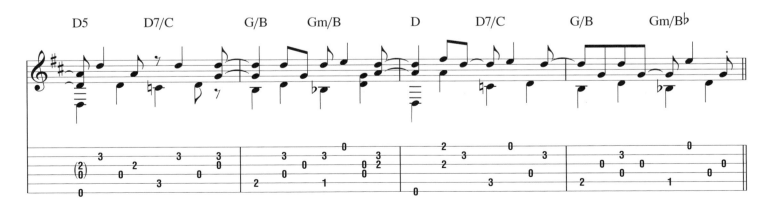

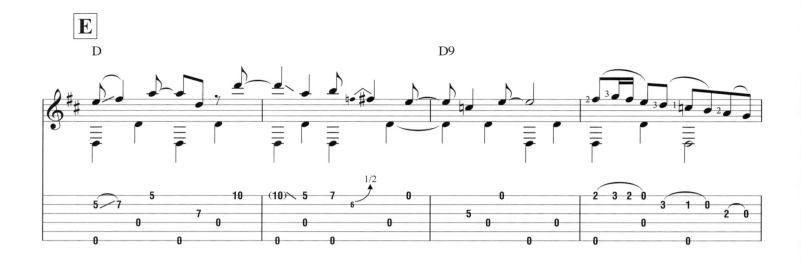

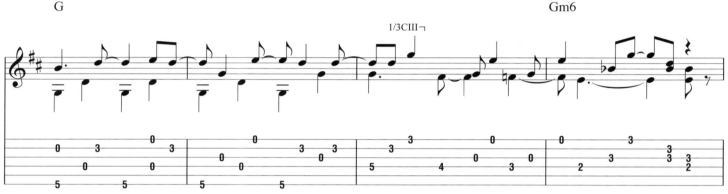

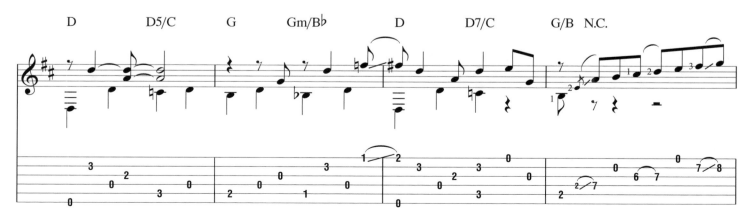

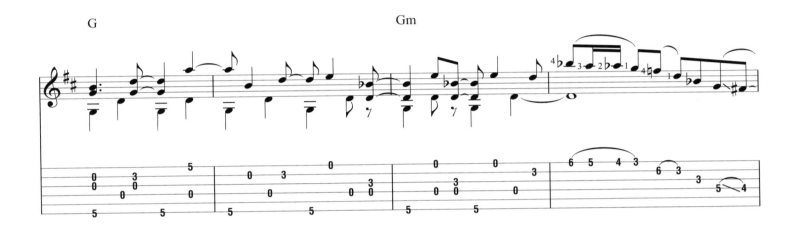

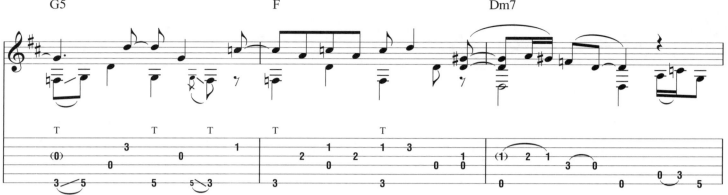

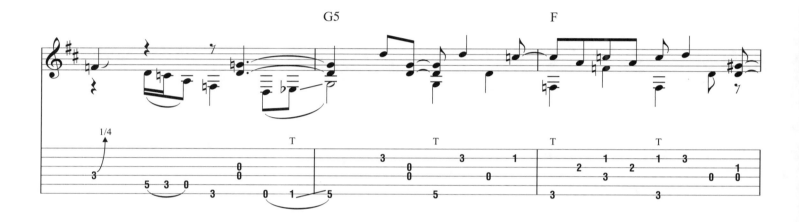

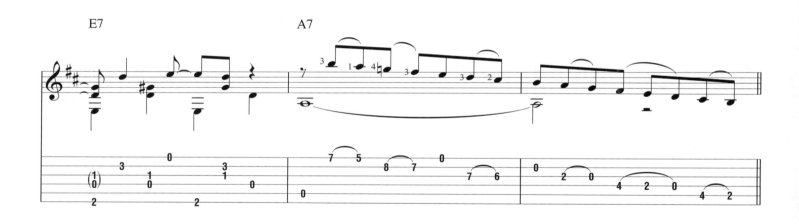

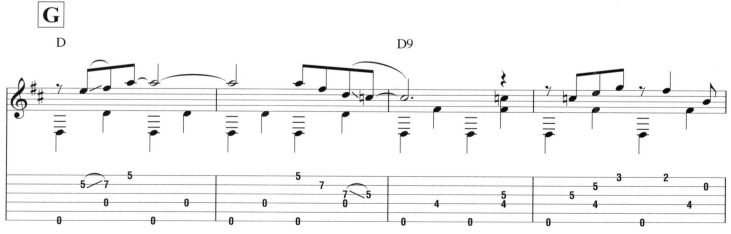

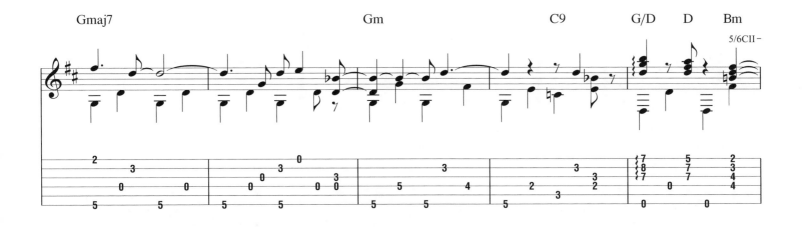

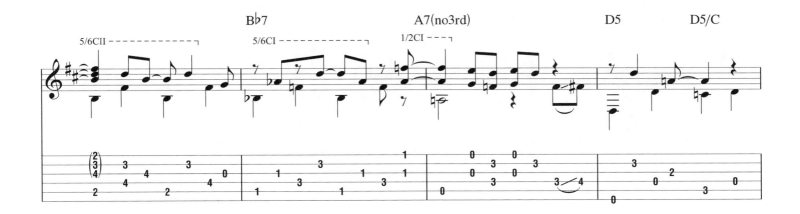

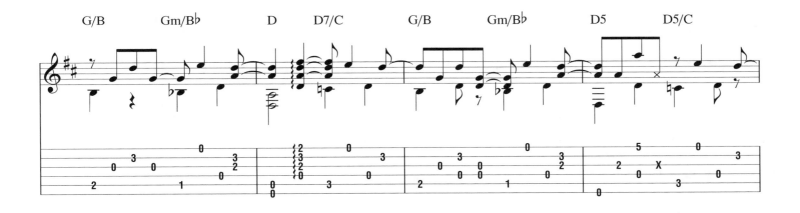

FINGERPICKING GUITAR BOOKS

Hone your fingerpicking skills with these great songbooks featuring solo guitar arrangements in standard notation and tablature. The arrangements in these books are carefully written for intermediate-level guitarists. Each song combines melody and harmony in one superb guitar fingerpicking arrangement. Each book also includes an introduction to basic fingerstyle guitar.

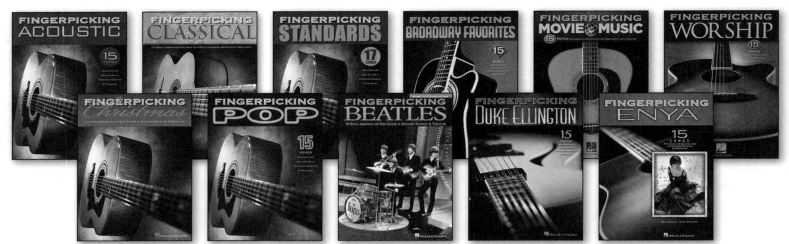

FINGERPICKING ACOUSTIC
00699614..$10.99

FINGERPICKING ACOUSTIC ROCK
00699764..$9.99

FINGERPICKING BACH
00699793..$8.95

FINGERPICKING BALLADS
00699717..$9.99

FINGERPICKING BEATLES
00699049..$19.99

FINGERPICKING BEETHOVEN
00702390..$7.99

FINGERPICKING BLUES
00701277 ....$7.99

FINGERPICKING BROADWAY FAVORITES
00699843..$9.99

FINGERPICKING BROADWAY HITS
00699838..$7.99

FINGERPICKING CELTIC FOLK
00701148..$7.99

FINGERPICKING CHILDREN'S SONGS
00699712..$9.99

FINGERPICKING CHRISTIAN
00701076 ....$7.99

FINGERPICKING CHRISTMAS
00699599..$8.95

FINGERPICKING CHRISTMAS CLASSICS
00701695..$7.99

FINGERPICKING CLASSICAL
00699620..$8.95

FINGERPICKING COUNTRY
00699687..$9.99

FINGERPICKING DISNEY
00699711..$10.99

FINGERPICKING DUKE ELLINGTON
00699845..$9.99

FINGERPICKING ENYA
00701161..$9.99

FINGERPICKING GOSPEL
00701059..$7.99

FINGERPICKING GUITAR BIBLE
00691040 ....$19.99

FINGERPICKING HYMNS
00699688..$8.95

FINGERPICKING IRISH SONGS
00701965..$7.99

FINGERPICKING JAZZ FAVORITES
00699844..$7.99

FINGERPICKING JAZZ STANDARDS
00699840..$7.99

FINGERPICKING LATIN FAVORITES
00699842..$9.99

FINGERPICKING LATIN STANDARDS
00699837..$7.99

FINGERPICKING ANDREW LLOYD WEBBER
00699839..$9.99

FINGERPICKING LOVE SONGS
00699841..$9.99

FINGERPICKING LOVE STANDARDS
00699836 ....$9.99

FINGERPICKING LULLABYES
00701276..$9.99

FINGERPICKING MOVIE MUSIC
00699919..$9.99

FINGERPICKING MOZART
00699794..$8.95

FINGERPICKING POP
00699615..$9.99

FINGERPICKING PRAISE
00699714..$8.95

FINGERPICKING ROCK
00699716..$9.99

FINGERPICKING STANDARDS
00699613..$9.99

FINGERPICKING WEDDING
00699637..$9.99

FINGERPICKING WORSHIP
00700554..$7.99

FINGERPICKING NEIL YOUNG – GREATEST HITS
00700134..$12.99

FINGERPICKING YULETIDE
00699654..$9.99

HAL•LEONARD®
CORPORATION

7777 W. BLUEMOUND RD. P.O. BOX 13819 MILWAUKEE, WI 53213

Visit Hal Leonard online at **www.halleonard.com**

Prices, contents and availability subject to change without notice.

JAZZ GUITAR CHORD MELODY SOLOS

This series features chord melody arrangements in standard notation and tablature of songs for intermediate guitarists.

ALL-TIME STANDARDS INCLUDES TAB
27 songs, including: All of Me • Bewitched • Come Fly with Me • A Fine Romance • Georgia on My Mind • How High the Moon • I'll Never Smile Again • I've Got You Under My Skin • It's De-Lovely • It's Only a Paper Moon • My Romance • Satin Doll • The Surrey with the Fringe on Top • Yesterdays • and more.
00699757 Solo Guitar $14.99

CHRISTMAS CAROLS INCLUDES TAB
26 songs, including: Auld Lang Syne • Away in a Manger • Deck the Hall • God Rest Ye Merry, Gentlemen • Good King Wenceslas • Here We Come A-Wassailing • It Came upon the Midnight Clear • Joy to the World • O Holy Night • O Little Town of Bethlehem • Silent Night • Toyland • We Three Kings of Orient Are • and more.
00701697 Solo Guitar $12.99

DISNEY SONGS INCLUDES TAB
27 songs, including: Beauty and the Beast • Can You Feel the Love Tonight • Candle on the Water • Colors of the Wind • A Dream Is a Wish Your Heart Makes • Heigh-Ho • Some Day My Prince Will Come • Under the Sea • When You Wish upon a Star • A Whole New World (Aladdin's Theme) • Zip-A-Dee-Doo-Dah • and more.
00701902 Solo Guitar $14.99

DUKE ELLINGTON INCLUDES TAB
25 songs, including: C-Jam Blues • Caravan • Do Nothin' Till You Hear from Me • Don't Get Around Much Anymore • I Got It Bad and That Ain't Good • I'm Just a Lucky So and So • In a Sentimental Mood • It Don't Mean a Thing (If It Ain't Got That Swing) • Mood Indigo • Perdido • Prelude to a Kiss • Satin Doll • and more.
00700636 Solo Guitar $12.99

FAVORITE STANDARDS INCLUDES TAB
27 songs, including: All the Way • Autumn in New York • Blue Skies • Cheek to Cheek • Don't Get Around Much Anymore • How Deep Is the Ocean • I'll Be Seeing You • Isn't It Romantic? • It Could Happen to You • The Lady Is a Tramp • Moon River • Speak Low • Take the "A" Train • Willow Weep for Me • Witchcraft • and more.
00699756 Solo Guitar $14.99

FINGERPICKING JAZZ STANDARDS INCLUDES TAB
15 songs: Autumn in New York • Body and Soul • Can't Help Lovin' Dat Man • Easy Living • A Fine Romance • Have You Met Miss Jones? • I'm Beginning to See the Light • It Could Happen to You • My Romance • Stella by Starlight • Tangerine • The Very Thought of You • The Way You Look Tonight • When Sunny Gets Blue • Yesterdays.
00699840 Solo Guitar $7.99

JAZZ BALLADS INCLUDES TAB
27 songs, including: Body and Soul • Darn That Dream • Easy to Love (You'd Be So Easy to Love) • Here's That Rainy Day • In a Sentimental Mood • Misty • My Foolish Heart • My Funny Valentine • The Nearness of You • Stella by Starlight • Time After Time • The Way You Look Tonight • When Sunny Gets Blue • and more.
00699755 Solo Guitar $14.99

JAZZ CLASSICS INCLUDES TAB
27 songs, including: Blue in Green • Bluesette • Bouncing with Bud • Cast Your Fate to the Wind • Con Alma • Doxy • Epistrophy • Footprints • Giant Steps • Invitation • Lullaby of Birdland • Lush Life • A Night in Tunisia • Nuages • Ruby, My Dear • St. Thomas • Stolen Moments • Waltz for Debby • Yardbird Suite • and more.
00699758 Solo Guitar $14.99

Prices, content, and availability subject to change without notice. | Disney characters and artwork ©Disney Enterprises, Inc.

"Well-crafted arrangements that sound great and are still accessible to most players."
— *Guitar Edge* magazine

HAL•LEONARD®
www.halleonard.com